The Rise of Islamic State

Patrick Cockburn is currently a Middle East correspondent for the *Independent* and worked previously for the *Financial Times*. He has written three books on Iraq's recent history, including *The Occupation: War and Resistance in Iraq*, which was a finalist for the National Book Critics' Circle Awards. He has written a memoir, *The Broken Boy*, and, with his son, a book on schizophrenia, *Henry's Demons*, which was shortlisted for a Costa Award. He won the Martha Gellhorn Prize in 2005, the James Cameron Prize in 2006, and the Orwell Prize for Journalism in 2009. He was named Foreign Commentator of the Year by the Comment Awards in 2013.

The Rise of Islamic State

ISIS and the New Sunni Revolution

Patrick Cockburn

VERSO
London • New York

First published under the title *The Jihadis Return*
by OR Books, New York and London 2014
This updated edition published by Verso 2015
© Patrick Cockburn 2014, 2015

7 9 10 8 6

Verso
UK: 6 Meard Street, London W1F 0EG
US: 20 Jay Street, Suite 1010, Brooklyn, NY 11201

www.versobooks.com

Verso is the imprint of New Left Books

ISBN-13: 978-1-78478-040-1
eISBN-13: 978-1-78478-049-4 (US)
eISBN-13: 978-1-78478-048-7 (UK)

British Library Cataloguing in Publication Data
A catalogue record for this book is available from the British Library

Library of Congress Cataloging-in-Publication Data

Cockburn, Patrick, 1950–
 The jihadi's return : ISIS and the failures of the global
war on terror / Patrick Cockburn.
  pages cm
 ISBN 978-1-78478-040-1 (paperback) — ISBN 978-
1-78478-049-4 (U.S.) — ISBN 978-1-78478-048-7
(U.K.)
1. IS (Organization) 2. Terrorism—Middle East.
3. Terrorism—Religious aspects—Islam. 4. Middle
East—History—21st century. I. Title.
HV6433.I722C64 2015
956.05'4—dc23

2014041837

Typeset in Fournier by MJ&N Gavan
Printed and bound by CPI Group (UK) Ltd, Croydon, CR0 4YY

Contents

Maps   vii
Preface: The Hundred Days   ix

1. The Rise of ISIS   1
2. The Battle of Mosul   11
3. In Denial   23
4. Jihadis on the March   41
5. The Sunni Resurgence in Iraq   61
6. Jihadis Hijack the Syria Uprising   79
7. Saudi Arabia Tries to Pull Back   97
8. If It Bleeds It Leads   111
9. Shock and War   135

Contents

Afterword   151
Acknowledgements   163
Index   165

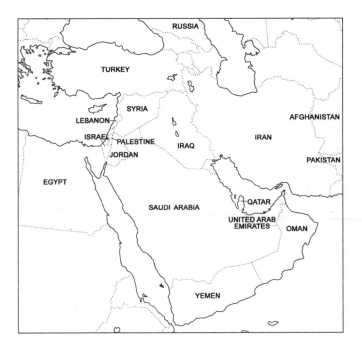

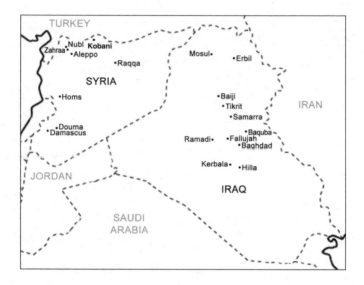

Preface: The Hundred Days

In the summer of 2014, over the course of one hundred days, the Islamic State of Iraq and the Levant (ISIS) transformed the politics of the Middle East. Jihadi fighters combined religious fanaticism and military expertise to win spectacular and unexpected victories against Iraqi, Syrian, and Kurdish forces. ISIS came to dominate the Sunni opposition to the governments in Iraq and Syria as it spread everywhere from Iraq's border with Iran to Iraqi Kurdistan and the outskirts of Aleppo, the largest city in Syria. During this rapid rise ISIS acted as though intoxicated by its own triumphs. It did not care about the lengthening list of its enemies, bringing together longtime rivals like the US and Iran by a common fear of the fundamentalists. Saudi Arabia and the Sunni monarchies of the Gulf joined in US air attacks on ISIS in Syria because they felt this group posed a greater threat to their own survival and the political status quo in the Middle East than anything they had seen since Saddam Hussein invaded Kuwait in 1990.

Iraq and Syria moved closer to disintegration as their diverse communities—Shia, Sunni, Kurds, Alawites, and Christians—found that they were fighting for their very existence. Merciless in enforcing compliance with its own exclusive and sectarian variant of Islam, ISIS killed or forced to flee all whom it targeted as "apostates" and "polytheists" or who were simply against its rule. Its leaders were the products of a decade of war in Iraq and Syria, and deliberate martyrdom through suicide bombing was a central and effective feature of their military tactics. The world had seen nothing like their use of public violence to terrorize their opponents since the Khmer Rouge in Cambodia forty years earlier.

The crucial date was June 10, 2014, when ISIS captured Iraq's northern capital Mosul after four days of fighting. On September 23, the US extended its use of airpower to Syria to prevent the jihadis' expansion. During the 105 days separating these two events ISIS rampaged through Iraq and Syria, defeating its enemies with ease even when they were more numerous and better equipped. Unsurprisingly, they attributed their victories to divine intervention.

In contrast, the Iraqi government had an army with 350,000 soldiers on which it had spent $41.6 billion in the three years since 2011. But this force melted away without significant resistance. Discarded uniforms and equipment were found strewn along the roads leading to Kurdistan and safety. Within two weeks those parts of northern and western Iraq outside Kurdish control were in the hands of ISIS. By the end of the month the new state had announced that it was establishing a caliphate reaching deep into Iraq and Syria. Its leader Abu Bakr al-Baghdadi said it was "a state where the Arab and non-Arab, the white man and black man, the easterner and westerner are all brothers ... Syria is not for the Syrians, and Iraq is not for the Iraqis. The Earth is Allah's."

Al-Baghdadi's words showed an intoxication with military victory that only increased as his men outfought and defeated opponents in Syria and Iraqi Kurdistan. The ISIS threat to the Kurdish capital Erbil in August provoked US air strikes inside Iraq, which were later extended to Syria on September 23. US airpower might not have been enough to eliminate or even contain

ISIS, but its use forced the fighters to abandon semi-conventional warfare conducted by flying columns of vehicles (often American Humvees captured from the Iraqi army) that were packed with heavily armed fighters. Instead ISIS has reverted to guerrilla warfare, no longer hoping to strike a swift knockout blow against Bashar al-Assad, the Syrian Kurds, or other Syria rebel groups that it had been fighting in an inter-rebel civil war since January 2014.

Over the course of those 100 days, the political geography of Iraq changed before its people's eyes and there were material signs of this everywhere. Baghdadis cook on propane gas because the electricity supply is so unreliable. Soon there was a chronic shortage of gas cylinders that came from Kirkuk; the road from the north had been cut by ISIS fighters. To hire a truck to come the 200 miles from the Kurdish capital Erbil to Baghdad now cost $10,000 for a single journey, compared to $500 a month earlier. There were ominous signs that Iraqis feared a future filled with violence as weapons and ammunition soared in price. The cost of a bullet for an AK-47 assault rifle quickly tripled to 3,000 Iraqi dinars, or about $2. Kalashnikovs were almost impossible to buy from arms dealers, though pistols could still be obtained at three times the price of the previous week. Suddenly, almost everybody had guns, including even Baghdad's paunchy, white-shirted traffic police, who began carrying submachine guns.

Many of the armed men who started appearing in the streets of Baghdad and other Shia cities were Shia militiamen, some from Asaib Ahl al-Haq, a dissident splinter group from the movement of the Shia populist nationalist cleric Muqtada al-Sadr. This organization was controlled by Prime Minister Nouri al-Maliki and the Iranians. It was a measure of the collapse of the state security forces and the national army that the government was relying on a sectarian militia to defend the capital. Ironically, up to this moment, one of Maliki's few achievements as prime minister had been to face down the Shia militias in 2008, but now he was encouraging them to return to the streets. Soon dead bodies were being dumped at night. They had been stripped of their ID cards but were assumed to be Sunni victims of the militia death squads. Iraq seemed to be slipping over the edge into an abyss in which sectarian massacres and countermassacres might rival those during the sectarian civil war between Sunni and Shia in 2006–7.

The hundred days of ISIS in 2014 mark the end of a distinct period in Iraqi history that began with the overthrow of Saddam Hussein by the US and British invasion of March 2003. Since then there has been an attempt by the Iraqi opposition to oust the old regime and their foreign allies and to create a new Iraq in which the three communities shared power in Baghdad. The experiment failed disastrously, and it seems it will be impossible to resurrect that project because the battle lines among Kurd, Sunni, and Shia are now too stark and embittered. The balance of power inside Iraq is changing. So too are the de facto frontiers of the state, with an expanded and increasingly independent Kurdistan—the Kurds having opportunistically used the crisis to secure territories they have always claimed—and the Iraqi-Syrian border having ceased to exist.

ISIS are experts in fear. The videos the group produces of its fighters executing Shia soldiers and truck drivers played an important role in terrifying and demoralizing Shia soldiers at the time of the capture of Mosul and Tikrit. Again, there were grim scenes uploaded to the Internet when ISIS routed the peshmerga (Kurdish soldiers) of the Kurdistan Regional Government in August. But fear has also brought together a great range of opponents of ISIS who were previously hostile to one another. In Iraq the US and Iranians are still publicly denouncing each other, but when Iranian-controlled Shia militias attacked north from Baghdad in September to end the ISIS siege of the Shia Turkoman town of Amerli, their advance was made possible by US air strikes on ISIS positions. When the discredited Iraqi prime minister Nouri al-Maliki was replaced by Haider al-Abadi during the same period, the change was backed by both Washington and Tehran. Maliki briefly considered resisting his displacement by mobilizing military units loyal to him in central Baghdad, but he was sharply warned against staging a coup by both Iranian and American officials.

Of course, American and Iranian spokesmen deny that there is active collaboration, but for the moment they are pursuing parallel policies towards ISIS, communicating their intentions through third parties and intelligence services. This is not exactly new: Iraqis have always said cynically that when it comes to Iraq, "the Iranians and the Americans shout at each other over the table, but shake hands under it." Such conspiracy theories can be carried too far, but it is true that, when it comes to relations between the US and its European allies on the one side, and Iran and the Syrian government on the other, there is a larger gap today than ever before between what Washington says and what it does.

The ISIS assault on the Kurds and, in particular, the Kurdish Yazidis in early August opened a new chapter in the history of American involvement in Iraq. The swift defeat of the peshmerga, supposedly superior fighters compared to the soldiers of the Iraqi army, was a fresh demonstration of ISIS's military prowess. Probably the military reputation of the peshmerga had been exaggerated: they had not fought anybody, aside from each other, for a quarter of a century, and an observer who knew them well always used to refer to them as the "pêche melba," adding that they were "only good for mountain ambushes." Jolted by the swift ISIS successes, the US intervened to launch air strikes to protect the Kurdish capital Erbil. From then on the US was back in the war, but reluctantly, and more aware than during the invasion of 2003 of the dangerous complexities of politics and warfare in Iraq. Again and again, President Obama and US officials said they needed a reliable partner in Baghdad, a more inclusive and less sectarian government than that of Maliki, if the US was to deploy its military might. Washington's aim was the sensible one of splitting the Sunni community off from ISIS and isolating the extremists, much as it had done during the "surge" in US troop numbers in 2007. The Americans argued that if at least part of the Iraqi Sunni community was to be conciliated, there had to be a government in Baghdad willing to share power, money, and jobs with the Sunni.

As so often in Iraq and Syria, this was easier said than done. Many of the Sunni living in the new caliphate did not like their new masters and were frightened of them. But they were even more frightened of the Iraqi army, the Shia militias, and the Kurds in Iraq, and the Syrian Army and the pro-Assad militias in Syria. The dilemma facing the Sunni in Iraq and Syria is graphically evoked in an email from a Sunni woman friend in Mosul, who has every reason to dislike ISIS, which was sent in September after her neighborhood was bombed by the Iraqi air force. It is worth quoting at length, as it shows how difficult it will be for the Iraqi Sunni to look on the government in Baghdad as anything but a hated enemy. She writes:

> The bombardment was carried out by the government. The air strikes focused on wholly civilian neighborhoods. Maybe they wanted to target two ISIS bases. But neither round of bombardment found its target. One target is a house connected to a church where ISIS men live. It is next to the neighborhood generator and about 200–300 meters from our home. The bombing hurt civilians only and demolished the generator. Now we don't have any electricity since yesterday night. I am writing from a device in my sister's house, which is empty. The government bombardment did not hit any of the ISIS men. I have just heard from a relative who visited us to check on us after that terrible night. He says that because of

this bombardment, youngsters are joining ISIS in tens if not in hundreds because this increases hatred towards the government, which doesn't care about us as Sunnis being killed and targeted. Government forces went to Amerli, a Shia village surrounded by tens of Sunni villages, though Amerli was never taken by ISIS. The government militias attacked the surrounding Sunni villages, killing hundreds, with help from the American air strikes.

Much the same is true of Syria. ISIS is more popular in the Sunni towns and villages they have captured around Aleppo than many other rebel groups that are halfway to being bandits. Here ISIS has been on the offensive and inflicted the most serious defeats the Syrian army has suffered in three years of war, capturing a well-defended air base at Tabqa in eastern Syria. Karen Koning AbuZayd, a member of the UN's Commission of Inquiry in Syria, said at that time that more and more Syrian rebels were defecting to ISIS: "They see it is better, these guys are strong, these guys are winning battles, they were taking money, they can train us."

US air strikes will inflict casualties on ISIS and make it more difficult for their columns of vehicles to move on the roads. But being the target of US planes also has advantages for them, because there will inevitably be civilian casualties. Airpower is no substitute for a reliable ally on the ground, and may be counterproductive in terms of alienating the local population. It may kill a number of ISIS fighters—but then many went to Iraq and Syria with the express intention of becoming martyrs. In early October the shortcomings of seeking to hold back ISIS by airpower alone were evident: its fighters were still advancing against the Syrian Kurds at Kobani and against Iraqi government forces west of Baghdad.

The political weakness of the US-led coalition was also becoming evident, because prominent members like Saudi Arabia, United Arab Emirates, and Turkey were as hostile to the Assad government, Syrian Kurds, and those fighting ISIS on the ground as they were to ISIS itself. US Vice President Joe Biden gave the US government's real view of its regional and Syrian allies with undiplomatic frankness when speaking at the John F. Kennedy Jr. Forum at Harvard University's Institute of Politics on October 2. He told his audience that Saudi Arabia, Turkey, and UAE

> were so determined to take down Assad and essentially have a proxy Sunni-Shia war. What did they do? They poured hundreds of millions of dollars and tens of thousands of tons of weapons into anyone who would fight against Assad, except that the people who were being supplied were al-Nusra and

al-Qaeda and the extremist elements of jihadis coming from other parts of the world.

He added that ISIS, under pressure in Iraq, had been able to rebuild its strength in Syria. As for the US policy of recruiting Syrian "moderates" to fight both ISIS and Assad, Biden said that in Syria the US had found "that there was no moderate middle because the moderate middle are made up of shopkeepers, not soldiers." Seldom have the real forces at work in creating ISIS and the present crisis in Iraq and Syria been so accurately described.

1

The Rise of ISIS

Today al-Qaeda–type movements rule a vast area in northern and western Iraq and eastern and northern Syria, several hundred times larger than any territory ever controlled by Osama bin Laden. It is since bin Laden's death that al-Qaeda affiliates or clones have had their greatest successes, including the capture of Raqqa in the eastern part of Syria, the only provincial capital in that country to fall to the rebels, in March 2013. In January 2014, ISIS took over Fallujah just forty miles west of Baghdad, a city famously besieged and stormed by US Marines ten years earlier. Within a few months they had also captured Mosul and Tikrit. The battle lines may continue to change, but the overall expansion of their power will be difficult to reverse. With their swift and multipronged assault across central and northern Iraq in June 2014, the ISIS militants had superseded al-Qaeda as the most powerful and effective jihadi group in the world.

These developments came as a shock to many in the West, including politicians and specialists whose view of what was happening often seemed outpaced by events. One reason for this was that it was too risky for journalists and outside observers to visit the areas where ISIS was operating, because of the extreme danger of being kidnapped or murdered. "Those who used to protect the foreign media can no longer protect themselves," one intrepid correspondent told me, explaining why he would not be returning to rebel-held Syria.

This lack of coverage had been convenient for the US and other Western governments because it enabled them to play down the extent to which the "war on terror" had failed so catastrophically in the years since 9/11. This failure is also masked by deceptions and self-deceptions on the part of governments. Speaking at West Point on America's role in the world on May 28, 2014, President Obama said that the main threat to the US no longer came from al-Qaeda central but from "decentralized al-Qaeda affiliates and extremists, many with agendas focused on the countries where they operate." He added that "as the Syrian civil war spills across borders, the capacity of battle-hardened extremist groups to come after us only increases." This was true enough, but Obama's solution to the danger was, as he put it, "to ramp up support for those in the Syrian opposition who offer the best alternative to terrorists." By June he was asking Congress for $500 million to train and equip "appropriately vetted" members of the Syrian opposition. It is here that there was a real intention to deceive, because, as Biden was to admit five months later, the Syrian military opposition is dominated by ISIS and by Jabhat al-Nusra, the official al-Qaeda representative, in addition to other extreme jihadi groups. In reality, there is no dividing wall between them and America's supposedly moderate opposition allies.

An intelligence officer from a Middle Eastern country neighboring Syria told me that ISIS members "say they are always pleased when sophisticated weapons are sent to anti-Assad groups of any kind, because they can always get the arms off them by threats of force or cash payments." These are not empty boasts. Arms supplied by US allies such as Saudi Arabia and Qatar to anti-Assad forces in Syria have been captured regularly in

Iraq. I experienced a small example of the consequences of this inflow of weapons even before the fall of Mosul, when, in the summer of 2014, I tried to book a flight to Baghdad on the same efficient European airline that I had used a year earlier. I was told it had discontinued flights to the Iraqi capital, because it feared that insurgents had obtained shoulder-held anti-aircraft missiles originally supplied to anti-Assad forces in Syria and would use them against commercial aircraft flying into Baghdad International Airport. Western support for the Syrian opposition may have failed to overthrow Assad, but it has been successful in destabilizing Iraq, as Iraqi politicians had long predicted.

The failure of the "war on terror" and the resurgence of al-Qaeda is further explained by a phenomenon which had become apparent within hours of the 9/11 attacks. The first moves from Washington made it clear that the anti-terror war would be waged without any confrontation with Saudi Arabia or Pakistan, two close US allies, despite the fact that without the involvement of these two countries 9/11 was unlikely to have happened. Of the nineteen hijackers that day, fifteen were Saudi. Bin Laden came from the Saudi elite. Subsequent US official documents stress repeatedly that financing for al-Qaeda and jihadi groups came from Saudi Arabia and the Gulf monarchies. As for Pakistan, its army and military service had played a central role since the early 1990s in propelling the Taliban into power in Afghanistan where they hosted bin Laden and al-Qaeda. After a brief hiatus during and after 9/11, Pakistan resumed its support for the Afghan Taliban. Speaking of the central role of Pakistan in backing the Taliban, the late Richard C. Holbrooke, US special representative to Afghanistan and Pakistan, said: "We may be fighting the wrong enemy in the wrong country."

The importance of Saudi Arabia in the rise and return of al-Qaeda is often misunderstood and under-stated. Saudi Arabia is influential because its oil and vast wealth make it powerful in the Middle East and beyond. But it is not financial resources alone that make it such an important player. Another factor is its propagating of Wahhabism, the fundamentalist, eighteenth-century version of Islam that imposes sharia law, relegates women to the status of second-class citizens, and regards Shia and Sufi Muslims as non-Muslims to be persecuted along with Christians and Jews.

This religious intolerance and political authoritari-anism, which in its readiness to use violence has many similarities with European fascism in the 1930s, is getting worse rather than better. For example, in recent years, a Saudi who set up a liberal website on which clerics could be criticized was sentenced to a thousand lashes and seven years in prison. The ideology of al-Qaeda and ISIS draws a great deal from Wahhabism. Critics of this new trend in Islam from elsewhere in the Muslim world do not survive long; they are forced to flee or are murdered. Denouncing jihadi leaders in Kabul in 2003, an Afghan editor described them as "holy fascists" who were misusing Islam as "an instrument to take over power." Unsurprisingly, he was accused of insulting Islam and had to leave the country.

A striking development in the Islamic world in recent decades is the way in which Wahhabism is taking over mainstream Sunni Islam. In one country after another Saudi Arabia is putting up the money for the training of preachers and the building of mosques. A result of this is the spread of sectarian strife between Sunni and Shia. The latter find themselves targeted with unprecedented viciousness, from Tunisia to Indonesia. Such sectarianism is not confined to country villages outside Aleppo or in the Punjab; it is poisoning relations between the two sects in every Islamic grouping. A Muslim friend in London told me: "Go through the address books of any Sunni or Shia in Britain and you will find very few names belonging to people outside their own community."

Even before Mosul, President Obama was coming to realize that al-Qaeda–type groups were far stronger than they had been previously, but his recipe for dealing with them repeats and exacerbates earlier mistakes. "We need partners to fight terrorists alongside us," he told his audience at West Point. But who are these partners going to be? Saudi Arabia and Qatar were not mentioned by him, since they remain close and active US allies in Syria. Obama instead singled out "Jordan and Lebanon, Turkey and Iraq" as partners to receive aid in "confronting terrorists working across Syria's borders."

There is something absurd about this, since the foreign jihadis in Syria and Iraq, the people whom Obama admits are the greatest threat, can only get to these countries because they are able to cross the 510-mile-long Turkish-Syrian border without hindrance from the Turkish authorities. Saudi Arabia, Turkey, and Jordan may now be frightened by the Frankenstein's monster they have helped to create, but there is little they can do to restrain it. An unspoken purpose of the US insistence that Saudi Arabia, UAE, Qatar, and Bahrain take part or assist in the air strikes on Syria in September was to force them to break their former links with the jihadis in Syria.

There was always something fantastical about the US and its Western allies teaming up with the theocratic

Sunni absolute monarchies of Saudi Arabia and the Gulf to spread democracy and enhance human rights in Syria, Iraq, and Libya. The US was a weaker power in the Middle East in 2011 than it had been in 2003, because its armies had failed to achieve their aims in Iraq and Afghanistan. Come the uprisings of 2011, it was the jihadi and Sunni-sectarian, militarized wing of rebel movements that received massive injections of money from the kings and emirs of the Gulf. The secular, non-sectarian opponents of the long-established police states were soon marginalized, reduced to silence, or killed. The international media was very slow to pick up on how the nature of these uprisings had changed, though the Islamists were very open about their sectarian priorities: in Libya, one of the first acts of the triumphant rebels was to call for the legalization of polygamy, which had been banned under the old regime.

ISIS is the child of war. Its members seek to reshape the world around them by acts of violence. The movement's toxic but potent mix of extreme religious beliefs and military skill is the outcome of the war in Iraq since the US invasion of 2003 and the war in Syria since 2011. Just as the violence in Iraq was ebbing, the war was revived by the Sunni Arabs in Syria. It is the government and media consensus in the West that the civil war in Iraq was reignited by the sectarian policies of Iraqi prime minister Nouri al-Maliki in Baghdad. In reality, it was the war in Syria that destabilized Iraq when jihadi groups like ISIS, then called al-Qaeda in Iraq, found a new battlefield where they could fight and flourish.

It was the US, Europe, and their regional allies in Turkey, Saudi Arabia, Qatar, Kuwait, and United Arab Emirates that created the conditions for the rise of ISIS. They kept the war going in Syria, though it was obvious from 2012 that Assad would not fall. He never controlled less than thirteen out of fourteen Syrian provincial capitals and was backed by Russia, Iran, and Hezbollah. Nevertheless, the only peace terms he was offered at the Geneva II peace talks in January 2014 was to leave power. He was not about to go, and ideal conditions were created for ISIS to prosper. The US and its allies are now trying to turn the Sunni communities in Iraq and Syria against the militants, but this will be difficult to do while these countries are convulsed by war.

The resurgence of al-Qaeda–type groups is not a threat confined to Syria, Iraq, and their near neighbors. What is happening in these countries, combined with the growing dominance of intolerant and exclusive Wahhabite beliefs within the worldwide Sunni community, means that all 1.6 billion Muslims, almost a quarter of the world's population, will be increasingly affected. It seems unlikely that non-Muslims, including many in the West, will be untouched by the conflict. Today's resurgent jihadism, having shifted the political terrain in Iraq and Syria, is already having far-reaching effects on global politics, with dire consequences for us all.

2

The Battle of Mosul

On June 6, 2014, ISIS fighters began an attack on Mosul, the second-largest city in Iraq. Four days later, the city fell. It was an astonishing victory by a force numbering some 1,300 men against a nominal 60,000-strong force including the Iraqi army and federal and local police. Like much else in Iraq, however, the disparity in numbers was not quite what it looked like. Such was the corruption in the Iraqi security forces that only about one in three of them was actually present in Mosul, the rest paying up to half their salaries to their officers to stay on permanent leave.

Mosul had long been highly insecure. Al-Qaeda in Iraq (as ISIS had formerly been known) had always maintained a strong presence in this overwhelmingly Sunni city of two million. For some time they had been able to extract protection money from businesses on a regular basis. In 2006 a businessman friend of mine in Baghdad told me that he was closing his cell phone shop in Mosul because of the payments he had to make to al-Qaeda. Exaggerated accounts of the success of the US troop surge the following year, which supposedly crushed al-Qaeda, ignored the militants' grip on Mosul. A few weeks after the fall of the city, I met a Turkish businessman in Baghdad who said that he had held a large construction contract in Mosul over the last few years. The local emir or leader of ISIS demanded $500,000 a month in protection money from his company. "I complained again and again to the government in Baghdad," the businessman said, "but they would do nothing about it except to say that I should add the money I paid to al-Qaeda to the contract price."

ISIS had another advantage, which has so far given it an edge over its many enemies. The Euphrates and Tigris river valleys, and the bleak steppe and desert where it operates in northern and western Iraq and eastern Syria, look very much the same whatever side of the border you are on. But the political and military conditions are wholly different in the two countries, enabling

ISIS commanders to move their forces back and forth between them, to take advantage of opportunities and to catch their enemies by surprise. Thus, ISIS took Mosul and Tikrit in June but did not attack Baghdad; in July it inflicted a series of defeats on the Syrian army; in August it stormed into Iraqi Kurdistan; and in September it was assaulting the Syrian Kurdish enclave at Kobani on the border with Turkey. ISIS was much strengthened by operating in two different countries.

The fall of Mosul in June 2014 is such a turning point in the history of Iraq, Syria, and the Middle East that it is worth describing in some detail how and why it fell.

In the lead-up to the siege, ISIS's campaign had begun with what appear as diversionary attacks on other targets in northern Iraq. This was probably a tactic to keep the Iraqi army and government in two minds for as long as possible about the real target. First, a column of vehicles packed with gunmen, and carrying heavy machine guns, smashed its way into Samarra in Salah ad-Din province on June 5 and seized much of the city. This was bound to elicit a strong government response because Samarra, though mostly Sunni, is the site of al-Askari, one of the holiest Shia shrines. A bomb attack in 2006 had led to a furious Shia response, with Sunni being massacred all over Baghdad. Predictably, the Iraqi army helicoptered in reinforcements from its elite Golden Division to drive out the enemy fighters. Other diversions included one in which gunmen seized part of the university campus at Ramadi, the capital of Anbar province, where hundreds of students were briefly held prisoner. In another at Baquba, northeast of Baghdad, a car bomb hit the counterterrorism bureau. Here, as elsewhere, the assault team did not press home their attacks and soon withdrew.

The attack on Mosul was much more serious, though this was not at first apparent. It began with five suicide bombings backed up by mortar fire. ISIS was joined by other Sunni paramilitary groups, including the Baathist Naqshbandi, Ansar al-Islam, and the Moujahideen Army, though how far these groups operated outside the authority of ISIS has been a matter of dispute. Jihadi fighters overran and tore down government checkpoints that had long paralyzed traffic in the city but proved useless as a security measure. These attacks were no different from those diversionary sorties launched further south, but on June 7 the US and the Kurdish Interior Ministry both detected a large ISIS convoy traveling from Syria towards Mosul. The next day's fighting was critical, as squads of ISIS fighters seized important buildings including the Federal Police headquarters. In

Baghdad the government wholly failed to comprehend the seriousness of the situation, telling worried US diplomats that it would take a week to send reinforcements to Mosul. It also turned down an offer by Massoud Barzani, the Kurdish leader, to send his peshmerga into Mosul to fight ISIS, considering it as an opportunistic land grab.

Defeat became irreversible on July 9, when three top Iraqi generals—Abboud Qanbar, the deputy chief of staff, Ali Ghaidan, the ground forces commander, and Mahdi Gharawi, the head of Nineveh Operations—climbed into a helicopter and fled to Kurdistan. This led to a final collapse of morale and the disintegration of the army forces. June 11 saw a reflection of the incapacity of the Maliki government to know what was happening or take a decision, when it granted approval for a peshmerga move into the city—a full day after it had fallen.

The story of one Iraqi Army soldier gives a sense of what it was like to be caught up in this shameful defeat. In early June, Abbas Saddam, a private soldier from a Shia district in Baghdad serving in the 11th Division of the Iraqi army, was transferred from Ramadi to Mosul. The fighting started not long after he got there. But on the morning of June 10 his commanding officer told the men to stop shooting, hand over their rifles to the insurgents, take off their uniforms, and get out of the city.

Before they could obey, their barracks were invaded by a crowd of civilians.

"They threw stones at us," Abbas recalled, "and shouted: 'We don't want you in our city! You are Maliki's sons! You are the sons of *mutta*! [the Shia tradition of temporary marriage much derided by Sunni] You are Safavids! You are the army of Iran!'"

The crowd's attack revealed that the fall of Mosul was the result of a popular uprising as well as a military assault. The Iraqi army was detested as a foreign occupying force of Shia soldiers, regarded in Mosul as creatures of an Iranian puppet regime led by Maliki. Abbas says there were ISIS fighters—called Daash in Iraq, after the Arabic acronym of their name—mixed in with the crowd. They said to the soldiers: "You guys are OK: just put up your rifles and go. If you don't, we'll kill you." Abbas saw women and children with military weapons; local people offered the soldiers dishdashes to replace their uniforms so that they could flee. He made his way back to his family in Baghdad, but didn't tell the army he was there for fear of being put on trial for desertion, as happened to a friend.

While the Sunni in Mosul were glad to see the back of the Iraqi army and terrified of its return, they were aware that Mosul had become a very dangerous place.

But there wasn't much they could do about it. On June 11 a woman friend, a Sunni with a professional job, sent an email that gives a sense of the anxieties shared by many. She wrote:

> Mosul has fallen completely into the hands of ISIS. The situation here is quite calm. They seem to be courteous with the people & they protect all the government establishments against looters. Mosul government & all the Iraqi army, police & security forces left their positions & fled the battle. We tried to flee to Kurdistan, but they won't allow us. They will put us as refugees in tents under the heat of the sun. So, the majority of the people just returned home & decided that they can't be refugees. But, we don't know what will happen in the following hours. May God protect everyone. Pray for us.

It was not only in Mosul that the Iraqi security forces disintegrated and fled, the rout led by their commanding officers. The town of Baiji, home to Iraq's largest refinery, gave up without a fight, as did Tikrit. Once again a helicopter appeared to take away army commanders and senior officials. In Tikrit soldiers who surrendered were divided into two groups—Sunni and Shia—and many of the latter were machine-gunned as they stood in front of a trench, their execution recorded on video to intimidate the remaining units of the Iraqi security forces. The

Americans said that five army and Federal Police divisions out of eighteen had disintegrated during the fall of northern Iraq. At the same time even ISIS seemed taken aback by the extent of their own success. "Enemies and supporters alike are flabbergasted," the ISIS spokesman Abu Mohammed al-Adnani declared. The boast nevertheless came with a warning that ISIS fighters should not be over-impressed by all the American-made military equipment they had captured. "Do not fall prey to your vanities and egos," he told them, but "march towards Baghdad" before the Shia could recover.

I arrived in Baghdad on June 16, when people were still in a state of shock following the collapse of the army. People could not quite believe that the period starting in 2005 when the Shia tried to dominate Iraq, as the Sunni had done under Saddam Hussein and the monarchy, was suddenly over. The disaster from their point of view was so unexpected and inexplicable that any other calamity seemed possible. The capital should have been secure: it had a Shia majority and was defended by the remains of the regular army, as well as tens of thousands of Shia militiamen. But then almost the same might have been said of Mosul and Tikrit.

The government's first reaction to defeat was disbelief and panic. Maliki blamed the fall of Mosul on a deep conspiracy, though he never identified the conspirators. He looked both baffled and defiant, but appeared to feel no personal responsibility for defeat—despite having personally appointed all fifteen of the army's divisional commanders.

In the first days after the fall of Mosul there was a sense of half-suppressed hysteria in the empty streets: people stayed at home, frightened, to follow the latest news on television. Many had stocked up on food and fuel within hours of hearing about the army's collapse. Sweetshops and bakeries make special pasties for breaking the fast at the end of the day during Ramadan, but few people were buying them. Weddings were cancelled. Rumors swept the city that ISIS was planning to make a sudden lunge into the center of Baghdad and storm the Green Zone, in spite of its immense fortifications. A Baghdad newspaper reported that no fewer than seven ministers and forty-two MPs had taken refuge in Jordan along with their families.

The biggest fear was that ISIS fighters, only an hour's drive away in Tikrit and Fallujah, would time their attack to coincide with an uprising in the capital's Sunni enclaves. The Sunni in Baghdad, though buoyed by the news of the fall of Sunni provinces to the insurgents, were afraid that the Shia would be tempted to carry out a pre-emptive massacre of the Sunni minority in the city as a potential fifth column. Sunni strongholds, like Adhamiya on the east bank of the Tigris, appeared to be deserted.

For example, I tried to hire a driver recommended by a friend. He told me he needed the money but he was a Sunni, and the risk of being stopped at a checkpoint was too great. "I am so frightened," he said, "that I always stay at home after six in the evening." It was easy to see what he meant. Sinister-looking men in civilian clothes, who might be from government intelligence or from the Shia militias, had suddenly appeared at police and army checkpoints, picking out suspects. These new plain-clothed officers were clearly in a position to give orders to the policemen and soldiers.

Sunni office workers asked to go home early to avoid being arrested; others stopped going to work. Being detained at a checkpoint carries an extra charge of fear in Baghdad because everybody, particularly the Sunni, remembers what it led to during the sectarian civil war of 2006–7: many of the checkpoints were run by death squads and the wrong ID card meant inevitable execution. Press reports claimed the killers were "men dressed as policemen," but everybody in Baghdad knows that policemen and militiamen are often interchangeable.

There was nothing paranoid or irrational about the ever-present sense of threat. Iraq's acting national security adviser, Safa Hussein, told me that "many people think" ISIS will "synchronize attacks from inside and outside Baghdad." He believed such an assault was possible, though he thought it would lead to defeat for ISIS and the Sunni rebels who joined them. The Sunni are in a minority, but it wouldn't take much for an attacking force coming from the Sunni heartlands in Anbar province to link up with districts in the city such as Amariya. For ISIS, seizing even part of Baghdad, one of the great Arab capitals and former seat of the Caliphate, would give credibility to its claim to be founding a new state.

3

In Denial

On August 8, the US Air Force started bombing ISIS in Iraq, and on September 23, the generals added ISIS and Jabhat al-Nusra, the al-Qaeda representative in Syria, to its targets. The militants, who had moved their men and equipment out of buildings and locations that could be easily hit, reverted to the guerrilla tactics that had served them well in the past.

In the US and Britain (which began air operations in Iraq on September 27), there was bombast about "degrading and destroying" ISIS, but there was no evidence of a long-term plan other than to contain and harass the jihadis by military means. As so often during the US military intervention in Iraq between 2003 and 2011, there was excessive focus by the media on the actions of Western governments as the prime mover of events. This was accompanied by an inadequate understanding of the significance of developments on the ground in Iraq and Syria as the force really driving the crisis in both countries.

Similarly, there was much joy in Western capitals when Iraq finally got rid of Nouri al-Maliki as prime minister and replaced him with Haider al-Abadi. The new administration was billed as more inclusive of Sunni Arabs and Kurds than under Maliki, but it was still dominated by the Dawa party, which had even more members in the cabinet than previously, and other Shia religious parties. Abadi promised the Sunni that there would be an end to the bombardment of Sunni civilian areas; but in one week in September Fallujah was shelled on six out of seven days, with twenty-eight civilians killed and 118 wounded, according to the local hospital.

The degree of political change was exaggerated, and not enough attention was given to the fact that Abadi, even with ISIS fighters a few miles from Baghdad, was unable to get the Iraqi parliament to approve his choices for the crucial posts of defense and interior ministers until October. Reidar Visser, the Norwegian expert on

Iraq, rated this failure as "far more significant than the plethora of international gatherings that are currently going on in the name of defeating ISIS in Iraq."

A pointer to the real state of affairs at this time was the outcome of a weeklong siege of an Iraqi army base at Saqlawiyah, just outside Fallujah, at the end of which ISIS fighters overran the position, killing or capturing most of the garrison. An Iraqi officer who escaped was quoted as saying that "of an estimated 1,000 soldiers in Saqlawiyah, only about 200 had managed to flee." ISIS said it had seized or destroyed five tanks and forty-one Humvees in liberating the area "from the filth of the Safavids [Shia]." Surviving Iraqi soldiers complained that during the siege they had received no reinforcements or supplies of ammunition, food or water, though they were only forty miles from Baghdad. In other words, three and a half months after the fall of Mosul and six weeks after the start of US air strikes, the Iraqi army was still unable to withstand an ISIS assault or carry out an elementary military operation. As at Mosul and Tikrit, the apparently Napoleonic successes of ISIS were partly explained by the incapacity of the Iraqi army.

In Syria the air strikes likewise led ISIS to revert to guerrilla-style operations, aside from two offensives it had launched in the north against Kurdish enclaves.

Some rebel units around Damascus, which had earlier given themselves Islamic-sounding names to attract Saudi and Gulf financing, opportunistically switched to more secular-sounding titles in a bid to attract American support. Jabhat al-Nusra, which, possibly to its own surprise, had been targeted by the US, condemned the American air raids and pledged common action with other jihadis against "the Crusaders." As in Iraq, it was not going to be easy to turn the Sunni and the rebels against ISIS now that the US was beginning to be seen as the de facto ally of Assad, whatever its protestations to the contrary.

In June many people in Baghdad had feared that ISIS would launch an assault on the capital, but the attack never came. As the attention of the world switched to a Malaysian aircraft shot down over Ukraine by Russian-supplied rebels and the Israeli bombardment of Gaza that killed 2,000 Palestinians, ISIS consolidated its position in the overwhelmingly Sunni Anbar province that sprawls across western Iraq. In Syria, it defeated or incorporated into its ranks other rebel groups and captured four different Syrian army bases, inflicting heavy casualties and taking much heavy equipment: the worst defeats suffered by the Damascus government in the whole of the uprising.

The newly declared caliphate was expanding by the day. It now covered an area larger than Great Britain and inhabited by some six million people—a population larger than that of Denmark, Finland, or Ireland. In a few weeks of fighting in Syria ISIS had established itself as the dominant force in the Syrian opposition, routing the official al-Qaeda affiliate, Jabhat al-Nusra, in the oil-rich province of Deir Ezzor and executing its local commander as he tried to flee. In northern Syria some 5,000 ISIS fighters were using tanks and artillery captured from the Iraqi army in Mosul to besiege half a million Kurds in their enclave at Kobani on the Turkish border. In central Syria, near Palmyra, ISIS fought the Syrian army as it overran the al-Shaer gas field, one of the largest in the country, in a surprise assault that left an estimated 300 soldiers and civilians dead. Repeated government counterattacks finally retook the gas field, but ISIS still controlled most of Syria's oil and gas production. The US Air Force was to concentrate on blowing up ISIS oil facilities when it started its bombardment; but a movement that claims to be fulfilling the will of God and makes a cult of martyrdom is not going to go out of business (or even be seriously demoralized) because of a shortage of cash.

The birth of the new state was the most radical change to the political geography of the Middle East since the

Sykes-Picot Agreement was implemented in the after-
math of the First World War. Yet at first this explosive
transformation created surprisingly little alarm internationally, or even among those in Iraq and Syria not yet
under the rule of ISIS. Politicians and diplomats tended
to treat ISIS as if it is a Bedouin raiding party that appears
dramatically from the desert, wins sweeping victories,
and then retreats to its strongholds, leaving the status
quo little changed. The very speed and unexpectedness
of its rise made it tempting for Western and regional
leaders to hope that the fall of ISIS and the implosion
of the caliphate might be equally sudden and swift. As
in any great disaster, people's moods gyrated between
panic and wishful thinking that the calamity was not as
bad as first imagined.

In Baghdad, with its mostly Shia population of seven
million, people knew what to expect should the mur-
derously anti-Shia ISIS forces capture the city, but they
took heart from the fact that it had not happened yet.
"We were frightened by the military disaster at first, but
we Baghdadis have got used to crises over the last thirty-
five years," one woman said. Even with ISIS at the gates,
Iraqi politicians went on playing political games as they
moved ponderously towards replacing the discredited
prime minister, Nouri al-Maliki.

"It is truly surreal," a former Iraqi minister said to me. "When you speak to any political leader in Baghdad they talk as if they had not just lost half the country." Volunteers had gone to the front after a fatwa from the grand ayatollah, Ali al-Sistani, Iraq's most influential Shia cleric. But by July these militiamen were streaming back to their homes, complaining that they were half-starved and forced to use their own weapons and buy their own ammunition. The only large-scale counter-attack launched by the regular army and the newly raised Shia militia was a disastrous foray into Tikrit on July 15 that was ambushed and defeated with heavy losses. There is no sign that the dysfunctional nature of the Iraqi army has changed. "They were using just one helicopter in support of the troops in Tikrit," the former minister said, "so I wonder what on earth happened to the 140 helicopters the Iraqi state has bought in recent years?" The answer probably was that the money for the missing 139 helicopters had simply been stolen.

In the face of these disasters the Shia majority took comfort from two beliefs that, if true, would mean the present situation was not as dangerous as it looked. They argued that Iraq's Sunnis had risen in revolt, and ISIS fighters were only the shock troops or vanguard of an uprising provoked by the anti-Sunni policies and actions of Maliki. Once he was replaced—as seemed inevitable given the pressure from Iran, America, and the Shia clerical hierarchy—Baghdad would offer the Sunnis a new power-sharing agreement with regional autonomy similar to that enjoyed by the Kurds. Then the Sunni tribes, former military officers, and Baathists who had allowed ISIS to take the lead in the Sunni revolt would turn on their ferocious allies. Despite the many signs to the contrary, Shia at all levels were putting faith in this comforting myth that ISIS was weak and could be easily discarded by Sunni moderates once they had achieved their goals. One Shia said to me: "I wonder if ISIS really exists."

Unfortunately, ISIS not only exists but is an efficient and ruthless organization that has no intention of waiting for its Sunni allies to betray it. In Mosul it demanded that all opposition fighters swear allegiance to the caliphate or give up their weapons. In late June and early July the militants detained former officers from Saddam Hussein's time, including two generals. Groups that had put up pictures of Saddam were told to take them down or face the consequences. "It doesn't seem likely," Aymenn al-Tamimi, an expert on jihadis, said, "that the rest of the Sunni military opposition will be able to turn against ISIS successfully. If they do, they will have to act as quickly as possible before ISIS gets too strong." He pointed out that the supposedly more moderate wing of the Sunni opposition had done nothing to stop the remnants of the ancient Christian community in Mosul from being forced to flee after ISIS told them they had to convert to Islam, pay a special tax, or be killed. Members of other sects and ethnic groups denounced as Shia or polytheists were being persecuted, imprisoned, and murdered. The moment seemed to be passing when the non-ISIS opposition could successfully mount a challenge.

The Iraqi Shia offered another explanation for the way their army disintegrated: it was stabbed in the back by the Kurds. Seeking to shift the blame from himself, Maliki claimed that Erbil, the Kurdish capital, "is a headquarters for ISIS, Baathists, al-Qaeda and terrorists." Many Shia believed this: it made them feel that their security forces (nominally 350,000 soldiers and 650,000 police) failed because they were betrayed, not because they would not fight. One Iraqi told me he was at an *iftar* meal during Ramadan "with a hundred Shia professional people, mostly doctors and engineers, and they all took the stab-in-the-back theory for granted as an explanation for what went wrong." The confrontation with the Kurds was important because it made it impossible to create a united front against ISIS: it showed how, even when faced by a common enemy, the Shia and Kurdish leaders could not cooperate. The Kurdish leader, Massoud Barzani, had taken advantage of the Iraqi army's flight to seize all the territories, including the city of Kirkuk, which have been in dispute between Kurds and Arabs since 2003. He now has a 600-mile common frontier with the caliphate and might have been an obvious ally for Baghdad, where Kurds make up part of the government. By trying to scapegoat the Kurds, Maliki ensured that the Shia would have no allies in their confrontation with ISIS if it resumed its attack in the direction of Baghdad. As for the Sunni, they were unlikely to be satisfied with regional autonomy for Sunni provinces and a larger share of jobs and oil revenues. Their uprising has been turned into a full counterrevolution that aims to take back power over all of Iraq.

In the roasting summer days of July, Baghdad had a phony-war atmosphere, like London or Paris in late 1939 or early 1940, and for similar reasons. People had feared an imminent battle for the capital after the fall of Mosul, but it had not happened yet and optimists hoped it would not happen at all. Life was more uncomfortable than it used to be, with only four hours of electricity on some days, but at least war had not yet come to the heart of the city. I went for dinner at the Alwiyah Club in central Baghdad and had difficulty in finding a table. Iraq's Shia leaders had not grasped that their domination over the Iraqi state, brought about by the US overthrow of Saddam Hussein, was finished, and only a Shia rump was left. It ended because of their own incompetence and corruption, and because the Sunni uprising in Syria in 2011 destabilized the sectarian balance of power in Iraq.

In Syria the ISIS-led Sunni victory in Iraq threatened to break the military stalemate. Assad had been slowly pushing back against a weakening opposition: in Damascus and its outskirts, the Qalamoun Mountains along the Lebanese border, and Homs, government forces had been advancing slowly and were close to encircling the large rebel enclave in Aleppo. But Assad's combat troops are noticeably thin on the ground, need to avoid heavy casualties, and only have the strength to fight on one front at a time. The government's tactic is to devastate a rebel-held district with artillery fire and barrel bombs dropped from helicopters, force most of the population to flee, seal off what may now be a sea of ruins, and ultimately force the rebels to surrender. But the arrival of large numbers of well-armed ISIS fighters fresh from recent successes was posing a new and dangerous challenge for Assad. A conspiracy theory much favored by the rest of the Syrian opposition and by Western diplomats, that ISIS and Assad are in league, was shown to be false as ISIS won victories on the battlefield. Likewise in Baghdad the conspiracy theory that ISIS was in league with the Kurds was dramatically blown away when ISIS launched their next surprise attack against Kurdish regions, defeated the peshmerga in Sinjar, forcing the Yazidis to flee, threatening the Kurdish capital Erbil, and provoking the re-entry of the US military into the Iraq war.

As ISIS became the largest force in the Syrian opposition it presented the West and its regional allies—Saudi Arabia, Qatar, UAE, and Turkey—with a quandary: their official policy was to get rid of Assad, but ISIS was now the second strongest military force in Syria; if he fell, it was in a good position to fill the vacuum. Like the Shia leaders in Baghdad, the US and its allies responded to the rise of ISIS by descending into fantasy. They pretended they were fostering a "third force" of moderate Syrian rebels to fight both Assad and ISIS, though in private Western diplomats admit that this group doesn't really exist outside a few beleaguered pockets. Aymenn al-Tamimi confirmed that this Western-backed opposition "is getting weaker and weaker"; he believes supplying them with more weapons won't make much difference. When US air strikes began the US did tell the Syrian government when and where they would be, but not the "moderate" rebels whom the US was publicly backing. The American military presumably calculated that anything they told the Free Syrian Army, the loose umbrella group of rebel units, would be known to ISIS and Jabhat al-Nusra within minutes.

Fear of ISIS grew internationally after the fall of Mosul, but only really became deep and pervasive when ISIS routed the Kurdish forces in Sinjar in early August and seemed poised to take the Kurdish capital Erbil. There was a sudden reordering of alliances and national priorities. As argued above, the foster-parents of ISIS and the other Sunni jihadi movements in Iraq and Syria had been Saudi Arabia, the Gulf monarchies, and Turkey. This doesn't mean the jihadis did not have strong indigenous roots, but their rise was crucially supported by outside Sunni powers. The Saudi and Qatari aid was primarily financial, usually through private donations, which Richard Dearlove, the former head of MI6, says were central to the ISIS takeover of Sunni provinces in northern Iraq: "Such things do not happen spontaneously." In a speech in London in July, he said the Saudi policy towards jihadis has two contradictory motives: fear of jihadis operating within Saudi Arabia, and a desire to use them against Shia powers abroad. He said the Saudis are "deeply attracted towards any militancy which can effectively challenge Shiadom." It is unlikely the Sunni community as a whole in Iraq would have lined up behind ISIS without the support Saudi Arabia gave directly or indirectly to many Sunni movements. The same is true of Syria, where Prince Bandar bin Sultan, the former Saudi ambassador to Washington and head of Saudi intelligence from 2012 to February 2014, had done everything he could to back the jihadi opposition until his dismissal. Fearful of what they've helped create, the Saudis now veered in the other direction, arresting jihadi volunteers rather than turning a blind eye as they go to Syria and Iraq, but it may be too late. Saudi jihadis have little love for the House of Saud. On July 23, ISIS launched an attack on one of the last Syrian army strongholds in the northern province of Raqqa. It began with a suicide car-bomb attack; the vehicle was driven by a Saudi called Khatab al-Najdi who had put pictures on the car windows of three women held in Saudi prisons, one of whom was Hila al-Kasir, his niece.

Turkey's role has been different but no less significant than Saudi Arabia's in aiding ISIS and other jihadi groups. Its most important action has been to keep open its 560-mile border with Syria. This gave ISIS, al-Nusra, and other opposition groups a safe rear base from which to bring in men and weapons. The border crossing points have been the most contested places during the rebels' "civil war within the civil war." Most foreign jihadis have crossed Turkey on their way to Syria and Iraq. Precise figures are difficult to come by, but Morocco's interior ministry said recently that 1,122 Moroccan jihadis have entered Syria, including 900 who went in 2013, 200 of whom were killed. Iraqi security suspects that Turkish military intelligence may have been heavily involved in aiding ISIS when it was reconstituting itself in 2011. Reports from the Turkish border say ISIS is no longer welcome, but with weapons taken from the Iraqi army and the seizure of Syrian oil and gas fields, it no longer needs so much outside help. The Turkish and Syrian Kurds accused Turkey of still being secretly hand-in-glove with ISIS, but this is probably an exaggeration. It would be truer to say that Turkey could see the advantages of ISIS weakening Assad and the Syrian Kurds. As the bombing of Syria began in September the US would boast of having assembled a coalition of forty states, but this loose alliance was not only unwieldy but had so many different agendas as to paralyze united action.

For America, Britain, and the Western powers, the rise of ISIS and the caliphate is the ultimate disaster. Whatever they intended by their invasion of Iraq in 2003 and their efforts to unseat Assad in Syria since 2011, it was not to see the creation of a jihadi state spanning northern Iraq and Syria, run by a movement a hundred times bigger and much better organized than the al-Qaeda of Osama bin Laden. The war on terror for which civil liberties have been curtailed and hundreds of billions of dollars spent has failed miserably. The belief that ISIS is interested only in "Muslim against Muslim" struggles is another instance of wishful thinking: ISIS has shown it will fight anybody who does not adhere to its bigoted, puritanical, and violent variant of Islam. Where ISIS differs from al-Qaeda is that it is a well-run military organization that is very careful in choosing its targets and the optimum moment to attack them.

Many in Baghdad hoped the excesses of ISIS—for example, blowing up mosques it deems shrines, like that of Younis (Jonah) in Mosul—will alienate the Sunnis. In the long term they may do just that as ISIS imposes its primeval religious and social norms throughout its territory. It is worth relating one incident from an ISIS-held area which illustrates the popular mood. The witness, a woman, relates:

Just this evening, with my old mom, I went out for shopping
and buying medicines in my car with a thin cloth showing my
eyes only. What can I do? Last week, a woman was standing
beside a kiosk, and uncovered her face drinking a bottle of
water. One of them [ISIS] approached her and hit her on the
head with a thick stick. He didn't recognize that her husband
was close to her. Her husband beat him up and he ran away
shooting randomly into the sky as the people, in sympathy,
chased him to share in beating him. This is just one story of
the brutality we are living.

In a land of heavy smokers, bonfires of cigarettes
arranged by ISIS are not popular. But opposing ISIS is
very dangerous and, for all its brutality, it has brought
victory to a crushed and persecuted Sunni community.
Even those Sunnis in Mosul who do not like it are fearful
of the return of a vengeful Shia-dominated Iraqi government. So far Baghdad's response to its defeat has
been to bomb Mosul and Tikrit randomly, leaving local
people in no doubt about its indifference to their welfare
or survival. The fear will not change even with Maliki
replaced by a more conciliatory prime minister. A Sunni
in Mosul, writing just after a missile fired by government forces had exploded in the city, told me: "Maliki's
forces have already demolished the University of Tikrit.
It has become havoc and rubble like all the city. If Maliki
reaches us in Mosul he will kill its people or turn them

into refugees. Pray for us." Such views are common, and make it less likely that Sunnis will rise up in opposition to ISIS and its caliphate. A new and terrifying state has been born that will not easily disappear.

4

Jihadis on the March

A video posted in the spring of 2014 by the Islamic
State of Iraq and the Levant (ISIS—formerly al-Qaeda
in Iraq) shows foreign jihadis, most likely somewhere
in Syria, burning their passports to demonstrate a
permanent commitment to jihad. The film, which is pro-
fessionally made, is sobering to watch for anybody who
imagines that the ongoing war in Syria can be contained.
It shows rather how the conflict in the great swath of territory between the Tigris River and the Mediterranean
coast is starting to convulse the entire region.

You can tell by the covers of the passports being
burned that most of them are Saudi, which are grass

green, or Jordanian, which are dark blue, though many other nationalities are represented in the group. As each man rips up his passport and throws it into the flames, he makes a declaration of faith, a promise to fight against the ruler of the country from which he comes. A Canadian makes a short speech in English and, before switching to Arabic, says: "[This] is a message to Canada and all American powers. We are coming and we will destroy you." A Jordanian says: "I say to the tyrant of Jordan: we are the descendants of Abu Musab al-Zarqawi [the Jordanian founding father of al-Qaeda in Iraq killed by US aircraft in 2006] and we are coming to kill you." A Saudi, an Egyptian, and a Chechen all make similar threats underlining the jihadis' open intention to operate anywhere in the world. What makes their threats particularly alarming is that their base area, the land where they are in control, is today larger by far than anything an al-Qaeda type of group has held before.

If you look at a map of the Middle East, you will find that al-Qaeda–type organizations have become a lethally powerful force in a territory that stretches from Diyala province northeast of Baghdad, to northern Latakia province on Syria's Mediterranean coastline. The whole of the Euphrates Valley through western Iraq, eastern Syria, and right up to the Turkish border is today under the rule of ISIS or Jabhat al-Nusra (JAN), the latter being the official representative of what US officials call "core" al-Qaeda in Pakistan. Al-Qaeda–type groups in western and northern Iraq and northern and eastern Syria now control a territory the size of Britain or Michigan, and the area in which they can mount operations is much bigger.

The Syrian-Iraqi border has largely ceased to exist. It is worth looking separately at the situation in the two countries, taking Iraq first. Here nearly all the Sunni areas, about a quarter of the country, are either wholly or partially controlled by ISIS. Before it captured Mosul and Tikrit it could field some 6,000 fighters, but this figure has multiplied many times since its gain in prestige and appeal to young Sunni men in the wake of its spectacular victories. Its very name (the Islamic State of Iraq and the Levant) expresses its intention: it plans to build an Islamic state in Iraq and in "al-Sham" or greater Syria. It is not planning to share power with anybody. Led since 2010 by Abu Bakr al-Baghdadi, also known as Abu Dua, it has proved itself even more violent and sectarian than the "core" al-Qaeda, led by Ayman al-Zawahiri, who is based in Pakistan.

Abu Bakr al-Baghdadi began to appear from the

shadows in the summer of 2010 when he became leader of al-Qaeda in Iraq (AQI) after its former leaders were killed in an attack by US and Iraqi troops. AQI was at a low point in its fortunes, as the Sunni rebellion, in which it had once played a leading role, was collapsing. It was revived by the revolt of the Sunni in Syria in 2011 and, over the next three years, by a series of carefully planned campaigns in both Iraq and Syria. How far al-Baghdadi has been directly responsible for the military strategy and tactics of AQI and later ISIS is uncertain: former Iraqi army and intelligence officers from the Saddam era are said to have played a crucial role, but are under al-Baghdadi's overall leadership.

Details of al-Baghdadi's career depend on whether the source is ISIS itself, or US or Iraqi intelligence, but the overall picture appears fairly clear. He was born in Samarra, a largely Sunni city north of Baghdad, in 1971 and is well educated, with degrees in Islamic studies, including poetry, history, and genealogy from the Islamic University of Baghdad. A picture of al-Baghdadi, taken when he was a prisoner of the Americans in Camp Bucca in southern Iraq, shows an average-looking Iraqi man in his mid-twenties with black hair and brown eyes.

His real name is believed to be Awwad Ibrahim Ali al-Badri al-Samarrai. He may have been an Islamic militant under Saddam as a preacher in Diyala province, to the northeast of Baghdad, where, after the US invasion of 2003, he had his own armed group. Insurgent movements have a strong motive for giving out misleading information about their command structure and leadership, but it appears al-Baghdadi spent five years, between 2005 and 2009, as prisoner of the Americans.

After he took over, AQI became increasingly well organized, even issuing detailed annual reports itemizing its operations in each Iraqi province. Recalling the fate of his predecessors as AQI leader, al-Baghdadi insisted on extreme secrecy, so few people knew where he was. AQI prisoners either say they never met him or, when they did, that he was wearing a mask.

Taking advantage of the Syrian civil war, al-Baghdadi sent experienced fighters and funds to Syria to set up JAN as the al-Qaeda affiliate in Syria. He split from it in 2013, but remained in control of a great swath of territory in northern Syria and Iraq.

Against fragmented and dysfunctional opposition, al-Baghdadi has moved fast towards establishing himself as an effective, albeit elusive, leader. The swift rise of ISIS since he took charge has been greatly helped by the uprising of the Sunni in Syria in 2011, which encouraged the six million Sunnis in Iraq to take a stand against the political and economic marginalization they have encountered since the fall of Saddam Hussein.

ISIS launched a well-planned campaign in 2013, including a successful assault on Abu Ghraib prison in the summer of that year to free its leaders and experienced fighters. The military sophistication of ISIS is far greater than the al-Qaeda organization from which it emerged, even at the peak of its success in 2006–7 before the Americans turned many of the Sunni tribes against it.

ISIS has the great advantage of being able to operate on both sides of the Syrian-Iraqi border. Though inside Syria ISIS is engaged in an intra-jihadi civil war with JAN, Ahrar al-Sham, and other groups, it still controls Raqqa and much of eastern Syria outside enclaves held by the Kurds close to the Turkish border. Jessica D. Lewis of the Institute for the Study of War, in a study of the jihadi movement at the end of 2013, described it as "an extremely vigorous, resilient and capable organization that can operate from Basra to coastal Syria." Though the swiftly growing power of ISIS was obvious to those who followed its fortunes, the significance of what was happening was taken on board by few foreign governments, hence the widespread shock that greeted the fall of Mosul.

In expanding its influence, ISIS has been able to capitalize on two factors: the Sunni revolt in neighboring Syria, and the alienation of the Iraqi Sunni by a Shia-led government in Baghdad. Protests by the Sunnis that started in December 2012 were initially peaceful. But a lack of concessions by Prime Minister Nouri al-Maliki together with a massacre at a peace camp at Hawijah in April 2013, which was stormed by the Iraqi army and resulted in the deaths of over fifty protestors, transmuted peaceful protest into armed resistance. In the parliamentary election of April 2014, Maliki presented himself primarily as the leader of the Shia who would quell a Sunni counterrevolution centered in Anbar. After Mosul, Maliki was blamed for refusing reform that might have blunted the appeal of ISIS, but he was not the only Shia leader who believed that the Sunni would never accept the loss of their old dominance.

The general Sunni hostility to Maliki as a proponent of sectarianism had enabled ISIS to ally itself with seven or eight Sunni militant groups with which it had previously been fighting. Mr. Maliki is not to blame for everything that has gone wrong in Iraq, but he played a central role in pushing the Sunni community into the arms of ISIS, something it may come to regret. Paradoxically, although he did well in the April 2014 parliamentary election by frightening the Shia voters with talk of a Sunni counterrevolution, he behaved as if this was merely an electoral ploy and seemed not to realize how close the Sunni were to an actual insurrection, using ISIS as their shock troops.

In this failing, he ignored some pretty obvious warning signs. At the start of 2014, ISIS had taken over Fallujah forty miles west of Baghdad as well as extensive territory in Anbar, the huge province encompassing much of western Iraq. In March, its gunmen paraded through Fallujah's streets to show off their recent capture of US-made armored Humvees from the Iraqi army. It was a final humiliation for the US that al-Qaeda's black flag should once again fly over a city that had been captured by US Marines in 2004 after a hard-fought victory accompanied by much self-congratulatory rhetoric. ISIS not only holds the city now, but also the nearby Fallujah dam, which allows them to regulate the flow of the Euphrates, either flooding or choking off the river for cities farther south. Unable to dislodge them by force, the Baghdad government diverted the water of the river into an old channel outside the control of the rebel fighters, which relieved the immediate crisis. But the fighting in Anbar showed how the military balance of power has changed in favor of ISIS. The Iraqi army, with five divisions stationed in the province, suffered a devastating defeat, reportedly losing 5,000 men dead and wounded and another 12,000 who deserted.

Farther to the north in June 2014, ISIS, joining forces with local Sunnis, took control of Mosul (Iraq's second-largest city with a population of over one million), swiftly ousting the Iraqi military from the city. But, as one Iraqi remarked, in some respects "Mosul had ceased to be under government authority long before." Prior to the takeover, ISIS had been levying taxes on everybody from vegetable sellers in the market to mobile phone and construction companies. By one estimate its income from this alone was $8 million (£4.8 million) a month. The same sort of "taxation" was occurring in Tikrit, north of Baghdad, where a friend reported that people would not eat at any restaurant that wasn't up to date with its tax payments to ISIS lest the place be bombed while they were dining.

Turning now to Syria: today the armed opposition to the Assad government is dominated by jihadis who wish to establish an Islamic state. They accept foreign fighters and have a vicious record of massacring Syria's minorities, notably the Alawites and the Christians. With the exception of those areas held by the Kurds, the whole eastern side of the country, including many of the Syrian oil fields, is now under jihadi control. The government clings to a few outposts in this vast area but does not have the forces to recapture it.

Different jihadi groups compete with each other in this region and, since early 2014, have been engaged in internecine combat. In 2012, ISIS founded JAN, sensing an opportunity during the rapidly escalating civil war in Syria and fearing that its own struggle might be marginalized. It sent the new group money, arms, and experienced fighters. A year later, it tried to reassert its authority over the fledgling group, which had become excessively independent in the eyes of ISIS leaders, attempting to fold it into a broader organization covering both Syria and Iraq. JAN resisted this effort, and the two groups became involved in a complicated intra-jihadi civil war. The Islamic Front, a newly established and powerful alliance of opposition brigades backed by Turkey and Qatar, is also fighting ISIS, despite sharing its aim of strict imposition of sharia. When it comes to social and religious mores, ISIS and JAN do not differ markedly, although the latter organization has a reputation for being less rigid. However, it was JAN fighters in Deir Ezzor on the Euphrates in eastern Syria who burst into a wedding party in a private house, beating and arresting women who were listening to loud music and not wearing Islamic dress.

Despite this conflict, non-jihadi groups are today peripheral in the Syrian opposition. In particular the more secular Free Syrian Army (FSA), whose political wing was once designated by the West as the next rulers of Syria, has been marginalized. ISIS holds eastern Aleppo province while much of the recent fighting in Aleppo city itself has been led by JAN and Ahrar al-Sham, another al-Qaeda–type movement. A recent attack on Syrian government–held territory in Latakia, located on the Mediterranean coast, was spearheaded by Morrocan jihadis along with Chechens. Meanwhile, JAN fighters run some of the suburbs of Damascus and a variety of villages and towns stretching up to the Turkish border. The fighting between ISIS and the other jihadis is really a battle over the spoils, more of a reflection of how strong they are than of any differences with respect to their long-term aims.

This sharp increase in the strength and reach of jihadist organizations in Syria and Iraq has generally been unacknowledged until recently by politicians and media in the West. A primary reason for this is that Western governments and their security forces narrowly define the jihadist threat as those forces directly controlled by al-Qaeda central or "core" al-Qaeda. This enables them to present a much more cheerful picture of their successes in the so-called "war on terror" than the situation on the ground warrants. In fact, the idea that the only jihadis to be worried about are those with the official blessing of al-Qaeda is naïve and self-deceiving. It ignores the fact, for instance, that ISIS has been criticized by the al-Qaeda leader Ayman al-Zawahiri for its excessive violence and sectarianism. After talking to a range of Syrian jihadi rebels not directly affiliated with al-Qaeda in southeast Turkey earlier this year, a source told me that "without exception they all expressed enthusiasm for the 9/11 attacks and hoped the same thing would happen in Europe as well as the US."

Jihadi groups ideologically close to al-Qaeda have been relabeled as moderate if their actions are deemed supportive of US policy aims. In Syria, the Americans backed a plan by Saudi Arabia to build up a "Southern Front" based in Jordan that would be hostile to the Assad government in Damascus, and simultaneously hostile to al-Qaeda–type rebels in the north and east. The powerful but supposedly moderate Yarmouk Brigade, reportedly the planned recipient of anti-aircraft missiles from Saudi Arabia, was intended to be the leading element in this new formation. But numerous videos show that the Yarmouk Brigade has frequently fought in collaboration with JAN, the official al-Qaeda affiliate. Since it was likely that, in the midst of battle, these two groups would share their munitions, Washington was effectively allowing advanced weaponry to be handed over to its deadliest enemy. Iraqi officials confirm that they have captured sophisticated arms from ISIS fighters in Iraq that were originally supplied by outside powers to forces considered to be anti-al-Qaeda in Syria.

The name al-Qaeda has always been applied flexibly when identifying an enemy. In 2003 and 2004 in Iraq, as armed Iraqi opposition to the American and British-led occupation mounted, US officials attributed most attacks to al-Qaeda, though many were carried out by national-ist and Baathist groups. Propaganda like this helped to persuade nearly 60 percent of US voters prior to the Iraq invasion that there was a connection between Saddam Hussein and those responsible for 9/11, despite the absence of any evidence for this. In Iraq itself, indeed throughout the entire Muslim world, these accusations have benefited al-Qaeda by exaggerating its role in the resistance to the US and British occupation.

Precisely the opposite PR tactics were employed by Western governments in 2011 in Libya, where any similarity between al-Qaeda and the NATO-backed rebels fighting to overthrow the Libyan leader, Muammar Gaddafi, was played down. Only those jihadis who had a direct operational link to the al-Qaeda "core" of Osama bin Laden were deemed to be dangerous. The falsity of the pretense that the anti-Gaddafi jihadis in Libya were less threatening than those in direct contact with al-Qaeda was forcefully, if tragically, exposed when US ambassador Chris Stevens was killed by jihadi fighters in Benghazi in September 2012. These were the same fighters lauded by Western governments and media for their role in the anti-Gaddafi uprising.

Al-Qaeda is an idea rather than an organization, and this has long been the case. For a five-year period after 1996, it did have cadres, resources, and camps in Afghanistan, but these were eliminated after the overthrow of the Taliban in 2001. Subsequently, al-Qaeda's name became primarily a rallying cry, a set of Islamic beliefs, centering on the creation of an Islamic state, the imposition of sharia, a return to Islamic customs, the subjugation of women, and the waging of holy war against other Muslims, notably the Shia, who are considered heretics worthy of death. At the center of this doctrine for making war is an emphasis on self-sacrifice and martyrdom as a symbol of religious faith and commitment.

This has resulted in using untrained but fanatical believers as suicide bombers, to devastating effect.

It has always been in the interest of the US and other governments that al-Qaeda be viewed as having a command-and-control structure like a mini-Pentagon, or like the mafia in America. This is a comforting image for the public because organized groups, however demonic, can be tracked down and eliminated through imprisonment or death. More alarming is the reality of a movement whose adherents are self-recruited and can spring up anywhere.

Osama bin Laden's gathering of militants, which he did not call al-Qaeda until after 9/11, was just one of many jihadi groups twelve years ago. But today its ideas and methods are predominant among jihadis because of the prestige and publicity it gained through the destruction of the Twin Towers, the war in Iraq, and its demonization by Washington as the source of all anti-American evil. These days, there is a narrowing of differences in the beliefs of jihadis, regardless of whether or not they are formally linked to al-Qaeda central.

Unsurprisingly, governments prefer the fantasy picture of al-Qaeda because it enables them to claim victories when it succeeds in killing its better-known members and allies. Often, those eliminated are given quasi-military ranks, such as "head of operations," to enhance the significance of their demise. The culmination of this heavily publicized but largely irrelevant aspect of the "war on terror" was the killing of bin Laden in Abbottabad in Pakistan in 2011. This enabled President Obama to grandstand before the American public as the man who had presided over the hunting down of al-Qaeda's leader. In practical terms, however, his death had little impact on al-Qaeda–type jihadi groups, whose greatest expansion has occurred subsequently.

The key decisions that enabled al-Qaeda to survive, and later to expand, were made in the hours immediately after 9/11. Almost every significant element in the project to crash planes into the Twin Towers and other iconic American buildings led back to Saudi Arabia. Bin Laden was a member of the Saudi elite, and his father had been a close associate of the Saudi monarch. Citing a CIA report from 2002, the official 9/11 report says that al-Qaeda relied for its financing on "a variety of donors and fundraisers, primarily in the Gulf countries and particularly in Saudi Arabia." The report's investigators repeatedly found their access limited or denied when seeking information in Saudi Arabia. Yet President George W. Bush apparently never even considered holding the Saudis responsible for what happened. An exit of senior Saudis, including bin Laden relatives, from the US was facilitated by the US government in the days after 9/11. Most significant, twenty-eight pages of the 9/11 Commission Report about the relationship between the attackers and Saudi Arabia were cut and never published, despite a promise by President Obama to do so, on the grounds of national security.

In 2009, eight years after 9/11, a cable from the US secretary of state, Hillary Clinton, revealed by WikiLeaks, complained that donors in Saudi Arabia constituted the most significant source of funding to Sunni terrorist groups worldwide. But despite this private admission, the US and Western Europeans continued to remain indifferent to Saudi preachers whose message, spread to millions by satellite TV, YouTube, and Twitter, called for the killing of the Shia as heretics. These calls came as al-Qaeda bombs were slaughtering people in Shia neighborhoods in Iraq. A sub-headline in another State Department cable in the same year reads: "Saudi Arabia: Anti-Shi'ism As Foreign Policy?" Now, five years later, Saudi-supported groups have a record of extreme sectarianism against non-Sunni Muslims. Pakistan, or rather Pakistani military intelligence in the shape of the Inter-Services Intelligence (ISI), was the other parent of al-Qaeda, the Taliban, and jihadi movements in general. When the Taliban was disintegrating under the weight of US bombing in 2001, its forces in northern Afghanistan were trapped by anti-Taliban forces. Before they surrendered, hundreds of ISI members, military trainers, and advisers were hastily evacuated by air. Despite the clearest evidence of ISI's sponsorship of the Taliban and jihadis in general, Washington refused to confront Pakistan, and thereby opened the way for the resurgence of the Taliban after 2003, which neither the US nor NATO has been able to reverse.

The "war on terror" has failed because it did not target the jihadi movement as a whole and, above all, was not aimed at Saudi Arabia and Pakistan, the two countries that fostered jihadism as a creed and a movement. The US did not do so because these countries were important American allies whom it did not want to offend. Saudi Arabia is an enormous market for American arms, and the Saudis have cultivated, and on occasion purchased, influential members of the American political establishment. Pakistan is a nuclear power with a population of 180 million and a military with close links to the Pentagon.

The spectacular resurgence of al-Qaeda and its offshoots has happened despite the huge expansion of

American and British intelligence services and their budgets after 9/11. Since then, the US, closely followed by Britain, has fought wars in Afghanistan and Iraq, and adopted procedures normally associated with police states, such as imprisonment without trial, rendition, torture, and domestic espionage. Governments wage the "war on terror" claiming that the rights of individual citizens must be sacrificed to secure the safety of all.

In the face of these controversial security measures, the movements against which they are aimed have not been defeated but rather have grown stronger. At the time of 9/11, al-Qaeda was a small, generally ineffectual organization; by 2014 al-Qaeda–type groups were numerous and powerful. In other words, the "war on terror," the waging of which has shaped the political landscape for so much of the world since 2001, has demonstrably failed. Until the fall of Mosul, nobody paid much attention.

5

The Sunni Resurgence in Iraq

In Iraq, events are not always what they seem. Take two recent occurrences that illustrate the difference between appearance and reality there. The first relates to the recapture of Fallujah in January 2014 by ISIS, aided by tribal militias. This was a body blow to the Iraqi government: Fallujah is only forty miles west of Baghdad; a famous Sunni stronghold; and a gateway to the capital. Soon after ISIS retook the city and reportedly stationed between 300 and 500 men armed with high-powered sniper rifles on its outskirts, government supporters circulated a reassuring video on Twitter and Facebook. It included some narrative in Iraqi Arabic, was shot from the air, and showed insurgents being targeted and eliminated by air-launched missiles. This was morale-raising stuff for government supporters. Unfortunately for them, within just a few hours of the video's first release, someone noticed that it had been shot in Afghanistan and was actually a video of American aircraft firing missiles at Taliban fighters. It is highly doubtful that Iraqi airpower is capable of carrying out such precision attacks; it later resorted to dropping random barrel bombs stuffed with explosives on Fallujah. The failure to take back Fallujah over a period of six months, and the need to invent even token victories for the Iraqi army, showed the real weakness of Iraq's million-strong security forces—350,000 soldiers and 650,000 police—something that was to be revealed even more starkly when ISIS swept away government authority across northern and western Iraq in June 2014.

Such deceptions are not all on the government side. A year previously, in December 2012, the arrest of the bodyguards of the moderate Sunni finance minister, Rafi al-Issawi, by the government led to widespread but peaceful protests in Sunni provinces in northern and central Iraq. Sunni Arabs make up about a fifth of Iraq's 33 million population. At first, the demonstrations were well attended, with protesters demanding an end to political, civil, and economic discrimination against the Sunni community. But soon they realized that Prime Minister Nouri al-Maliki was offering only cosmetic changes and many stopped attending the weekly demonstrations.

In the Sunni city of Tikrit, capital of Salah ad-Din province, 10,000 people had at first come to rallies, but the number then sank to just 1,000. A local observer reported: "It was decided that all mosques should be shut on Fridays except for one, forcing all the faithful to go to the same mosque for Friday prayers. Cameras eagerly filmed and photographed the crowd to make it look like they were all protesters and the images were beamed back to the Gulf, where their paymasters were fooled (or maybe they weren't) into thinking that the protests were still attracting large numbers." The eyewitness in Tikrit suggests cynically that the money supposedly spent on feeding and transporting nonexistent demonstrators was pocketed by protest leaders. The message was not that the Sunni were less angry than before but that peaceful protest was mutating into armed resistance.

These two stories illustrate an important political truth about contemporary Iraq: neither the government nor any of the constitutional political movements are as strong as they pretend to be. Power is divided, and these divisions have helped ISIS to emerge far stronger and more speedily in Iraq than anybody expected.

Though ISIS had gained momentum and notoriety leading up to June 2014, their victory in Mosul came as a major surprise—even to ISIS itself. "Enemies and supporters alike are flabbergasted," said ISIS spokesman Abu Mohammed al-Adnani. It is difficult to think of any examples in history when security forces a million strong, including fifteen divisions, have crumbled so quickly after attacks from an enemy force that has been estimated at 6,000. Key to making this possible was the fact that the Sunni population as a whole, sensing that an end to its oppression was at hand, was prepared to lend at least their tacit support.

The lack of morale and discipline in the Iraqi army was evidently also a major factor. Asked about the Iraqi military's cause of defeat, one recently retired Iraqi general was emphatic: "Corruption! Corruption! Corruption!" It started, he said, when the Americans told the Iraqi army to outsource food and other supplies around 2005. A battalion commander was paid for a unit of 600 soldiers, but had only 200 men under arms and pocketed the difference, which meant enormous profits. The army became a money-making machine for senior officers and often an extortion racket for ordinary soldiers who manned the checkpoints. On top of this, well-trained Sunni officers were sidelined. "Iraq did not really have a national army," the general concluded.

Corruption in the military took place at every level. A general could become a divisional commander at a cost of $2 million and would then have to recoup his investment from kickbacks at checkpoints on the roads, charging every goods vehicle that passed through. An Iraqi businessman told me some years ago that he had stopped importing goods through Basra port because the amount of money he had to spend bribing officials and soldiers at every stage as his goods were moved from the ship at the dockside to Baghdad made it unprofitable.

Another friend in Baghdad (I am afraid any account of Iraq will always be littered with sources who wish to remain anonymous) told me: "Soldiers under Saddam Hussein often wanted to desert—they were scarcely paid. But they knew they would be killed if they did, so it was better to die in battle. The present army has never been a national army. Its soldiers were only interested in their salaries and they were no longer frightened of what would happen to them if they ran away."

* * *

Iraqis are not naïve. The grim experiences of their country's rulers over the past fifty years have led many to recognize them as being self-serving, greedy, brutal, and incompetent. Ten years ago, some had hopes that they might escape living in a permanent state of emergency as the US and Britain prepared to overthrow Saddam Hussein. Others were wary of Iraqis returning from abroad who promised to build a new nation.

A few months before the 2003 invasion and occupation, an Iraqi civil servant secretly interviewed in Baghdad made a gloomy forecast. "The exiled Iraqis are the exact replica of those who currently govern us ... with the sole difference that the latter are already satiated since they have been robbing us for the past thirty years," he said. "Those who accompany the US troops will be ravenous."

Many of the Iraqis who came back to Iraq after the US-led invasion were people of high principle who had sacrificed much as opponents of Saddam Hussein. But fast-forward a decade and the prediction of the unnamed civil servant about the rapaciousness of Iraq's new government turns out to have been all too true. As one former minister put it, "the Iraqi government is an institutionalized kleptocracy."

"The corruption is unbelievable," said political

scientist and activist Ghassan al-Attiyah. "You can't get a job in the army unless you pay; you can't even get out of prison unless you pay. Maybe a judge sets you free but you must pay for the paperwork, otherwise you stay there. Even if you are free you may be captured by some officer who paid $10,000 to $50,000 for his job and needs to get the money back." In an Iraqi version of catch-22, everything is for sale. A former prison detainee said he had to pay his guards $100 for a single shower. Racketeering was, and continues to be, the norm: one entrepreneur built his house on top of a buried oil pipeline, drilled into it, and siphoned off quantities of fuel.

Corruption complicates and poisons the daily life of Iraqis, especially those who can afford to pay. But the frequent demand for bribes has not in itself crippled the state or the economy. The highly autonomous Kurdistan Regional Government is deemed extremely corrupt, but its economy is booming and its economic management is praised as a model for the country. More damaging for Iraq has been the wholesale theft of public funds. Despite tens of billions of dollars being spent, there is a continued shortage of electricity and other necessities. Few Iraqis regret the fall of Saddam, but many recall that, after the devastating US air strikes on the infrastructure in 1991, power stations were patched up quickly using only Iraqi resources.

There is more to Iraqi corruption than the stealing of oil revenues by a criminalized caste of politicians, parties, and officials. Critics of Prime Minster Maliki, who has been in power since 2006, say his method of political control has been to allocate contracts to supporters, wavering friends, or opponents whom he wants to win over. But that is not the end of the matter. Beneficiaries of this largesse have been "threatened with investigation and exposure if they step out of line," said one Iraqi observer. Even those who had not been awarded contracts knew that they were vulnerable to being targeted by anticorruption bodies. "Maliki uses files on his enemies like J. Edgar Hoover," the observer said. The government cannot reform the system because it would be striking at the very mechanism by which it rules. State institutions for combating corruption have been systematically defanged, marginalized, or intimidated. Why has the corruption in Iraq been so bad? The simple answer that Iraqis give is that "UN sanctions destroyed Iraqi society in the 1990s and the Americans destroyed the Iraqi state after 2003." Under Maliki's Shia-dominated government, patronage based on party, family, or community determines who gets a job, contributing further to the political and economic marginalization of Iraq's Sunni population that began after the fall of Saddam Hussein.

It is evident that ISIS has been able to exploit the growing sense of alienation and persecution among the Sunni in Iraq. "Belittled, demonized, and increasingly subject to a central government crackdown, the popular movement is slowly mutating into an armed struggle," reports the International Crisis Group. "Many Sunni Arabs have concluded that their only realistic option is a violent conflict increasingly framed in confessional terms." In other words, they see their best chance of surviving and even winning the struggle for power in Iraq is to fight as Sunnis against Shia hegemony.

The Shia-dominated government might have gotten away with its confrontational approach before 2011. But when the predominant theme of the Arab Spring uprising in Syria took the form of a revolt by the Sunni majority backed by Saudi Arabia and the Sunni monarchies of the Gulf and Turkey, the sectarian balance of power in the region began to change.

Previously, the Iraqi Sunni had been resentful but largely resigned to the Shia-Kurdish domination of Iraq established in 2003. They were fearful of a renewed onslaught by Shia militias and Shia-controlled security forces, which had driven the Sunni out of much of Baghdad in the sectarian civil war of 2006 and 2007.

A US embassy cable in September 2007 said: "More than half of all Baghdad neighborhoods now contain a clear Shia majority. Sunnis have largely fled to outlying areas or have been concentrated into small enclaves surrounded by Shia neighborhoods." To a great extent, this remains true today.

The shifting power dynamic along sectarian lines, most evident in the wake of the events of June 2014, also spurred fearful reactions from Iraq's Shia community. "The Shia in Iraq see what is happening not as the Sunni reacting justifiably against the government oppressing them but as an attempt to re-establish the old Sunni-dominated-type government," said one observer in the capital. On both the Shia and Sunni sides tensions had accumulated to the extent that a full-scale and bloody sectarian confrontation was inevitable.

The surge of young Shia men into militias in the summer of 2014 was touched off by an appeal of Grand Ayatollah Ali al-Sistani, the revered Shia cleric, for people to sign up. "The street is boiling," said one observer. Some 1,000 volunteers left Kerbala for the frontline city of Samarra, the site of the al-Askari mosque, one of the holiest Shia shrines in a city where the majority of the population is Sunni.

This polarization between the two religious groups was only intensified by the hot and cold war between the US and Russia. Proxies were at play here with Saudi Arabia and the Gulf monarchies, backed by the US, facing off against Iran, Syria, and Hezbollah in Lebanon, supported by Russia. Iranian President Hassan Rouhani, whose government has backed the Shia-led Iraqi state, pledged support for Maliki against the Sunni uprising, saying, "Iran will apply all its efforts on the international and regional levels to confront terrorism." With a long border in common, Iraq is Iran's most important ally, more important even than Syria. The Iranians were horrified by the sudden Iraqi military collapse, which created problems for Iran in Syria, where it had been struggling with some success to stabilize the rule of President Assad. Responding to the surge of ISIS control in Iraq in 2014, a cadre of advisers from the Iranian Revolutionary Guard Corps was believed to be putting together a new military force drawn from the army and militias.

Iraq has long suspected the hidden hand of Wahhabism, the variant of Islam espoused by Saudi Arabia, as being behind much of its troubles. In March 2014, Prime Minister Maliki, during an interview with France 24 television, put the blame squarely on Saudi Arabia and Qatar for the rise of Sunni violence in his country, saying that "these two countries are primarily responsible for the sectarian, terrorist and security crisis in Iraq."

He added that allegations that he was marginalizing Sunnis were broadcast by "sectarians with ties to foreign agendas, with Saudi and Qatari incitement." His accusations were angry and direct, alleging that Riyadh and Doha were providing support for the militants, including "buying weapons for the benefit of these terrorist organizations."

There was considerable truth in Maliki's charges. A proportion of aid from the Gulf destined for the armed opposition in Syria undoubtedly goes to jihadist militants in Iraq. Turkey allows weapons and jihadist volunteers, many of them potential suicide bombers, to cross its 510-mile-long border into Syria. Inevitably some of the guns, fighters, and bombers go to Iraq. This is hardly surprising given that ISIS operates in both countries as if they were one.

Over the past two years, violence has increased sharply, with nearly 10,000 Iraqi civilians killed in 2013 and almost 5,000 in just the first five months of 2014, according to Iraq Body Count. A senior US administration official, speaking in August 2013 and quoted by Jessica D. Lewis of the Institute for the Study of War, said: "We've had an average of about five to ten suicide bombers a month … We've seen over the [past] ninety days the suicide bomber numbers approach about thirty a month, and we still suspect that most of them are coming in from Syria."

A blind spot for the US and other Western powers has been their failure to see that by supporting the armed uprising in Syria, they would inevitably destabilize Iraq and provoke a new round of its sectarian civil war. Al-Qaeda in Iraq, as it was then known, was at its lowest ebb in 2010. It had been vigorously pursued by the Americans and was under attack from the Sahwa or "Awakening" groups of anti–al-Qaeda fighters, mostly drawn from the Sunni tribes. It had lost many of its veterans, who were dead or in prison, and survivors were unpopular among ordinary Sunnis because of their general bloodthirstiness, killing even minor government employees who might be Sunni. Above all, it had failed to overthrow the Shia-Kurdish government. Up to 2012, many Sunnis were hopeful of extracting at least some concessions from the government without going back to war.

The spectacular resurgence of the jihadists in Iraq came through a well-planned campaign, an important element of which was systematic attacks on the prisons. Known as the "Breaking the Walls" campaign, this involved eight separate attacks to free prisoners, culminating in a successful assault on Abu Ghraib and Taji prisons in the summer of 2013 when at least 500 captives, many of them experienced fighters, escaped. The attackers fired one hundred mortar bombs into the jails and used suicide bombers to clear the way as inmates rioted and started fires to confuse the guards.

Throughout 2013, ISIS attacks on security forces all over Iraq escalated. An assault by government forces on a peace camp at Hawijah, southwest of Kirkuk, on April 23 killed fifty people and injured 110, alienating many Sunni, including powerful tribes. Ill-planned government counteroffensives, which often meant detaining and mistreating all Sunni men of military age, proved counter-effective. Sporadic shelling of Fallujah and Ramadi by government forces in Anbar forced some 500,000 people out of a total population of 1.6 million in the province to flee to safer places where they often had to live rough or with whole families crammed into a single room.

All along the upper Euphrates River, food became

scarce and expensive and many schools were closed. The most important Sunni religious leader in Anbar, Abdul Malik al-Saadi, who had previously counseled moderation, insisted that the April 2014 parliamentary elections were illegitimate.

In the months leading up to its general offensive in June 2014, there was some uncertainty about the degree of control ISIS had over Sunni areas. Sometimes it chose to advertise its strength and sometimes not. Its takeover of Mosul, and the ease with which it occurred, was clearly a major symbolic victory for the jihadists, showing both their own effectiveness and the fragility of Iraq's enormous security forces.

However, the details of what precisely happened in the city remain cloudy because of a lack of reliable reporting on the ground, something that is unsurprising given the assassination campaign against local media that had taken place. Five journalists were killed in the six months after October 2013 and forty others had fled to Kurdistan and Turkey. Mukhtars, community leaders who are often the most important of the government's representatives, were also attacked, forcing them to flee the city or to cooperate with ISIS. Minorities such as the Yazidis and Christians were targeted as well.

Mosul is of particular importance to ISIS because it was the home of many families that joined the Iraqi army under Saddam Hussein, who traditionally picked his defense minister from the city. Brutal as ISIS fighters may be, for many in Mosul they are preferable to Maliki's Shia-dominant government forces. ISIS has been careful not to alienate the local population. ISIS spokesperson Abu Mohammed al-Adnani warned fighters to behave moderately towards the Sunni population, even those who may previously have fought on the government side. "Accept repentance and recantations from those who are sincere, and do not bother those who do not bother you, and forgive your Sunni folk, and be gentle with your tribes," he said. It remains to be seen if this approach will work. Mosul is a traditional, conservative city, but not an intensely religious one, and it is difficult to imagine ISIS ruling it without creating friction.

The surge in ISIS control in Sunni Iraq has happened rapidly, and there is little sign thus far of an effective government counterattack. The slaughter of Shia civilians continues, with a suicide bomber in a minivan packed with explosives killing 45 and wounding 157 people at a security checkpoint at the entrance to the largely Shia town of Hilla, southwest of Baghdad, as recently as March 2014. Government security is incapable of finding and eliminating the hideouts where these devastating vehicle-born bombs are rigged.

There may be another less obvious reason for the spectacular resurgence of ISIS. According to one senior Iraqi source, the reemergence of ISIS was significantly aided in 2011 and 2012 by Turkish military intelligence that encouraged experienced Iraqi officers, who may have participated in guerrilla war against the US occupation, to work with the movement. This might be dismissed as one more Middle East conspiracy theory, but a feature of jihadi-type movements is the ease with which they can be manipulated by foreign intelligence services.

Speaking of Iraq early in 2013, Dr. Mahmoud Othman, the veteran MP, said that "about half the country is not really controlled by the government." Asked why Iraq's one-million-strong security forces had been so ineffective against the jihadists, another politician, who did not want to be named, said: "This is the harvest of total corruption. People pay money to get into the army [so they can get a salary]—but they are investors not soldiers." These are harsh words, but evidence of their truth is provided by the fact that ISIS is now holding a large part of the country and the Iraqi army appears powerless to do anything about it.

6

Jihadists Hijack the Syria Uprising

Just after the sarin poison gas attacks on rebel-held districts of Damascus in August 2013, I appeared on an American television program with Razan Zaitouneh, a human rights lawyer and founder of the Violations Documentation Center, who was speaking via Skype from the opposition stronghold of Douma in East Damascus.

She gave a compelling, passionate, and wholly believable account of what had happened. "I have never seen so much death in my whole life," she said, describing people breaking down the doors of houses to find that everybody inside had been killed. Doctors in the few medical centers wept as they tried in vain to treat gas victims with the scarce medicines they had. Bodies, fifteen to twenty at a time, were being tipped into mass graves. She contemptuously dismissed any idea that the rebels might be behind the use of sarin, asking: "Do you think we are such crazy people that we would kill our own children?"

Zaitouneh had been defending political prisoners for a dozen years and was the sort of credible advocate that won the Syrian opposition so much international support in its first years. But on December 8, 2013, gunmen burst into her office in Douma and kidnapped her, along with her husband, Wael Hamada, and two civil rights activists: Samira al-Khalil, a lawyer, and Nazem al-Hamadi, a poet. None of the four has been heard from since. Although it denies any involvement, the group suspected of being behind the kidnapping is the Army of Islam, a group strong in rebel-held districts of Damascus that was created by Saudi Arabia as a jihadi counterbalance to JAN. Al-Khalil's husband, Yassin al-Haj Saleh, told the online publication al-Monitor: "Razan and Samira were part of a national inclusive secular movement and this led them to collide with the Islamist factions, who are inclined towards despotism."

The kidnapping and disappearance of Ms. Zaitouneh

and the others have many parallels elsewhere in Syria, where Islamists have killed civil rights activists or forced them to flee. Usually, this has happened when the activists have criticized them for killings, torture, imprisonment, or other crimes. Revolutions are notorious for devouring their earliest and most humane advocates, but few have done so with the speed and ferocity of Syria's.

Why has the Syrian uprising, whose early supporters demanded that tyranny should be replaced by a secular, nonsectarian, law-bound, and democratic state, failed so completely to achieve these aims? Syria has descended into a nightmarish sectarian civil war as the government bombs its own cities as if they were enemy territory and the armed opposition is dominated by Salafi-jihadist fighters who slaughter Alawites and Christians simply because of their religion. Syrians have to choose between a violent dictatorship, in which power is monopolized by the presidency and brutish security services, or an opposition that shoots children in the face for minor blasphemy and sends pictures of decapitated soldiers to the parents of their victims.

Syria today is like Lebanon during the fifteen-year-long civil war between 1975 and 1990. I was recently in Homs, once a city known for its vibrant diversity but now full of "ghost neighborhoods" where all the buildings are abandoned, smashed by shellfire or bombs. Walls still standing are so full of small holes from machine-gun fire that they look as if giant woodworms have been eating into the concrete.

This is a land of checkpoints, blockades, and sieges, during which the government seals off and bombards rebel-held enclaves. The strategy is working, but at a snail's pace that leaves much of Syria in ruins.

Aleppo, once the largest city in the country, is mostly depopulated. Government forces are advancing but are overstretched and cannot re-conquer northern and eastern Syria unless Turkey shuts its long border. Government success only strengthens the jihadists relative to other more moderate forces because they have a hardened core of fighters who will never surrender. So, as the Syrian army advances behind a barrage of barrel bombs in Aleppo, its troops are mostly fighting JAN, the official al-Qaeda affiliate, and the Salafist Ahrar al-Sham, backed by Qatar and Turkey. It is trying to repeat its success in parts of Damascus and Homs where it has sealed off and besieged rebel enclaves until making agreements which have approximated surrender. In contrast, the rebel enclave in the east of Aleppo city is more substantial, and closer to both the rebel heartland and the Turkish border. Its fall would mean the beginning of the end for the revolt, something its foreign backers do not wish to happen.

The degenerate state of the Syrian revolution stems from the country's deep political, religious, and economic divisions before 2011 and the way in which these have since been exploited and exacerbated by foreign intervention. The first protests happened when they did because of the uprisings of the "Arab Spring" in Tunisia, Egypt, Libya, Yemen, and Bahrain. They spread rapidly because of overreaction by state security forces firing on peaceful demonstrators, thereby enraging whole communities and provoking armed resistance. The government insists that protests were not as peaceful as they looked and that from an early stage their forces came under armed attack. There is some truth to this, but if the opposition's aim was to trap the government into a counterproductive punitive response, it has succeeded beyond its dreams.

Syria was always a less coherent society than it looked to outside observers, and its divisions were not just along religious lines. In July 2011, the Brussels-based International Crisis Group (ICG) wrote in a report: "The Syrian authorities claim they are fighting a foreign-sponsored, Islamist conspiracy, when for the most part they have been waging war against their original social constituency. When it first came to power, the Assad regime embodied the neglected countryside, its peasants and exploited underclass. Today's ruling elite has forgotten its roots."

In the four years of drought before 2011, the United Nations noted that up to three million Syrian farmers had been pushed into "extreme poverty" and had fled the countryside to squat in shanty towns on the outskirts of the cities. Middle-class salaries could not keep up with inflation. Cheap imports, often from Turkey, forced small manufacturers out of business and helped to pauperize the urban working class. The state was in contact with whole areas of life in Syria solely through corrupt and predatory security services. The ICG conceded that there was "an Islamist undercurrent to the uprising" but it was not the main motivation for the peaceful protests that were mutating into military conflict.

Compare this analysis of the situation in the summer of 2011 with what happened three years later. By 2014, the war had reached a stalemate and the armed opposition was dominated by ISIS. Ideologically, there was not much difference between ISIS and other jihadist groups in the opposition such as Ahrar al-Sham or the Army of Islam, which also seek a theocratic Sunni state under sharia law. Pilloried in the West for their sectarian ferocity, these jihadists were often welcomed by local people for restoring law and order after the looting and banditry of the Western-backed Free Syrian Army (FSA), the loose umbrella group to which, at one time, 1,200 rebel bands owed nominal allegiance. In Afghanistan in the 1990s, the iron rule of the Taliban had been initially welcomed by many for the same reason.

The degree to which the armed opposition was under the thumb of foreign backers at the end of 2013 is well illustrated by the confessions of Saddam al-Jamal, a brigade leader in the Ahfad al-Rasoul Brigade and the former FSA commander in eastern Syria. A fascinating interview with Jamal, conducted by ISIS and translated by the Brown Moses blog, was recorded after he had defected to ISIS. Ignoring his self-serving denunciations of the un-Islamic actions of his former FSA associates, the interview appears to be reliable. He speaks as if it was matter of course that his own group, al-Ahfad, was funded by one or the other of the Gulf monarchies: "At the beginning of the Syrian revolution, the file was handled by Qatar. After a while, they switched to Saudi Arabia."

Jamal says meetings of the FSA military council were invariably attended by representatives of the Saudi, UAE, Jordanian, and Qatari intelligence services, as well as intelligence officers from the US, Britain, and France. At one such meeting, apparently in Ankara, Jamal says the Saudi deputy defence minister, Prince Salman bin Sultan, the half brother of Saudi intelligence chief Bandar bin Sultan, addressed them all and asked Syrian leaders of the armed opposition "who have plans to attack Assad positions to present their needs for arms, ammo and money." The impression one gets is of a movement wholly controlled by Arab and Western intelligence agencies. It may be a measure of Saudi recognition of how dramatically the plan to overthrow Assad failed that Bandar and Salman have now both lost their jobs.

The civil war between jihadist groups that started with a coordinated attack on ISIS positions in January 2014 is damaging the standing of all of them. Foreign fighters who came to Syria to fight Assad and the Shia find they are being told to kill Sunni jihadists with exactly the same ideological views as themselves.

ISIS sent the suicide bomber who killed Abdullah Muhammad al-Muhaysani, the official al-Qaeda representative in Syria and also a leader of Ahrar al-Sham. This is evidence of how al-Qaeda central has links at different levels to jihadi organizations with which it is not formally associated. Attempts by Saudi Arabia, the US, and Jordan to build up a "Southern Front" of insurgents who are both anti-Assad and anti–al-Qaeda have so far failed, in part because of Jordanian reservations about becoming too visible as combatants.

Returning jihadists are finding their route home is not always an easy one, since their native governments, for example in Saudi Arabia or Tunisia, which may have welcomed their departure as a way of exporting dangerous fanatics, are now appalled by the idea of battle-hardened Salafists coming back. An activist in the northern Syrian city of Raqqa, seeking to speed the departure of Tunisian volunteers, showed them a video of bikini-clad women on Tunisian beaches and suggested that their puritanical presence was needed back home to prevent such loose practices.

It is a measure of Syria's descent into apocalyptic violence that the official representative of al-Qaeda there, JAN, should now be deemed more moderate than ISIS. The latter retreated earlier in 2014 but this may have been a tactical move while it prepared its offensive in northern Iraq. It has a vast territory in eastern Syria and western Iraq where it can regroup and plan counterattacks. In any case, JAN has always sought mediation with ISIS and does not generally want a fight. The jihadist civil war has made life easier for the government militarily, since its enemies are busy killing each other, but it also does not have the resources to fully eliminate them. It will soon be facing an emboldened ISIS fresh from its victories in Iraq and eager to show that it can do the same in Syria.

Many mistakes have been made about Syria by both the outside world and the opposition since 2011, but perhaps the most serious was the belief that President Assad was going to go down in defeat like Muammar Gaddafi in Libya. Both the rebels and their foreign backers forgot that Gaddafi was largely overthrown by the NATO air campaign. Without NATO, the rebels would not have lasted more than a few weeks. But the belief that Assad was weak only began to be treated skeptically in 2013. In 2012, foreign governments and foreign journalists were speculating what place he might choose for exile, even though he still held all fourteen Syrian provincial capitals. ISIS now controls one of them, Raqqa on the Euphrates, but the main population centers are still held by the government. A problem here for the nonjihadi opposition was that their whole strategy, insofar as they had one, was based on creating another Libya-type situation. When that failed to materialize, they had no plan B.

Though Assad—like the opposition in 2011 and 2012—may overestimate the strength of the cards he holds, the political and military terrain today looks much more positive from his point of view. The army, the pro-Assad militias, and allies like Hezbollah are extending their grip on Damascus, on the Qalamoun Mountains along the Lebanese border, and in Homs City and province. They are, however, achieving these gains very slowly, which betrays the government's shortage of effective combat troops and its need to avoid casualties. The overweight draftees manning checkpoints do not look as if they want to fight anybody. Rather than taking over rebel-held areas, the government simply bombards them so that the civilian population is forced to flee and those who remain are either families of fighters or those too poor to find anywhere else to live. Electricity and water is then cut off and a siege is mounted. In Adra on the northern outskirts of Damascus in early 2014, I witnessed JAN forces storm a housing complex by advancing through a drainage pipe which came out behind government lines, where they proceeded to kill Alawites and Christians. The government did not counterattack but simply continued its siege.

There are many local ceasefires in these areas which are not far from being surrenders. I was in one district called Barzeh where the FSA fighters kept their weapons, and where a rebel commander told me "we were expecting them to release 350 prisoners from Barzeh but all we have got so far is three dead bodies." He asked me, rather despairingly, if I knew anybody in Syrian military intelligence who might know what had happened to them.

The political landscape of Syria is much more variegated than it looks from the outside. For instance, in February 2014 in a town called Nabq on the Damascus-Homs road, which had just been recaptured, government forces organized a victory celebration guarded by their militia, the National Defence Force (NDF). However, local people told me that the rebels, who a week earlier had informed them they would all fight to the last bullet against Assad's forces, were now all members of the NDF.

This pattern is repeated all the way up to Homs and then east along the Syrian border where the rebels have been losing villages or strong points like Krak des Chevaliers. Homs City itself has been under government control for some time, with the exception of a big area called al-Waer in the northwest, where several hundred thousand Sunni have taken refuge. The similarities between the situation in Homs province and

Lebanon during the civil war are striking. Around Krak des Chevaliers, for instance, Christian villages are to be found next to Turkoman Sunni communities and, closer to the border with Lebanon, there are houses with statues of the Virgin Mary outside the door, indicating that the occupants are Maronites.

The farther north one travels, the less progress is being made by the government forces. Of course, here the rebels have the enormous advantage of the proximity of a border with Turkey that is essentially open to myriad smuggling operations, both commercial and military. Significantly, many of the intra-rebel battles have been fought over the control of border crossings that can be used to move men and weapons, and to provide a source of revenue.

Wide swaths of the country are devastated. The whole north of Damascus, for instance, looks like a picture of Stalingrad, where the buildings are blasted beyond repair or bulldozed. Refugees are not returning; there isn't anything to come back to. The government does not offer much by way of reconciliation either. Politically, its main argument is that "at least we are better than the other side who chop off people's heads if they belong to a different religion or sect." This obviously frightens Alawites, Christians, Kurds, and others, but it also frightens Sunnis who work for the government. The great weakness of the opposition is the degree to which it has allowed or encouraged the conflict to become a vicious sectarian war. Christian opposition women are forced to wear the veil and dissenters are threatened by punishment of death. An important factor in the Syrian war, which makes it different from previous conflicts, is that the threat of death or torture by the other side is all the more terrifying since Syrians can see myriad examples of such atrocities on the Internet. People who relate to their opponents largely through snuff movies are unlikely to be in a mood to compromise.

What could be done to end all of this? The theory that arming the opposition will bring Assad to discuss peace and his own departure presupposes a complete transformation of the situation on the battlefield. This would only happen, if at all, after years of fighting. It also presumes that Russia, Iran, and Hezbollah are willing to see their Syrian ally defeated. Given that the insurgency is now dominated by ISIS, JAN, and other al-Qaeda–type groups, it is unlikely that even Washington, London, and Riyadh now want to see Assad fall. But allowing Assad to win would be seen as a defeat for the West and their Arab and Turkish allies. "They climbed too far up the tree claiming Assad has to be replaced to reverse their policy now," says one former Syrian minister. By insisting that Assad should go as a precondition of peace, while knowing this is not going to happen, his enemies are in practice ensuring that the war will go on. Assad may not want a peaceful compromise, but then neither is he being offered one.

If the war cannot be ended, could its impact on the Syrian people be mitigated? Given the current level of violence, negotiations are smothered at birth by what was once called in Northern Ireland "the politics of the last atrocity." Hatred and fear are too deep for anybody to risk being seen making concessions. And, in any case, one must question whether JAN or ISIS are in the business of negotiating with anybody. Certainly, until recently, the answer seemed to be firmly negative. But in May 2014, the last 1,200 fighters and their weapons were evacuated from the Old City of Homs, while food was allowed into two Shia towns, Nubl and Zahraa outside Aleppo, by the besieging rebels. Pro-Assad captives were released elsewhere. Such local agreements and truces are becoming increasingly possible because of war weariness. They are unlikely to be more than temporary. However, as one observer in Beirut put it: "There were over 600 ceasefires in the Lebanese civil war. They were always fragile and people laughed at them but they saved a lot of lives."

The Syrian crisis comprises five different conflicts that cross-infect and exacerbate each other. The war commenced with a genuine popular revolt against a brutal and corrupt dictatorship, but it soon became intertwined with the struggle of the Sunni against the Alawites, and that fed into the Shia-Sunni conflict in the region as a whole, with a standoff between the US, Saudi Arabia, and the Sunni states on the one side and Iran, Iraq, and the Lebanese Shia on the other. In addition to this, there is a revived cold war between Moscow and the West, exacerbated by the conflict in Libya and more recently made even worse by the crisis in the Ukraine.

The conflict has become like a Middle East version of the Thirty Years' War in Germany four hundred years ago. Too many players are fighting each other for different reasons for all of them to be satisfied by peace terms and to be willing to lay down their arms at the same time. Some still think they can win and others simply want to avoid a defeat. In Syria, as in Germany between 1618 and 1648, all sides exaggerate their own strength and imagine that temporary success on the battlefield will open the way to total victory. Many Syrians now see the outcome of their civil war resting largely with the US, Russia, Saudi Arabia, and Iran. In this, they are probably right.

7

Saudi Arabia Tries to Pull Back

A chilling five-minute film made by ISIS shows its fighters stopping three large trucks on what looks like the main highway linking Syria and Iraq. A burly, bearded gunman inspects the ID cards of the drivers who stand nervously in front of him.

"You are all Shia," he says threateningly.

"No, we are Sunni from Homs," says one of the drivers in a low, hopeless tone of voice. "May Allah give you victory."

"We just want to live," pleads another driver. "We are here because we want to earn a living." The ISIS man puts them through a test to see if they are Sunni. "How many times do you kneel for the dawn prayer?" he asks. Their answers vary between three and five.

"What are the Alawites doing with the honor of Syria?" rhetorically asks the gunman who by this stage has been joined by other fighters. "They are raping women and killing Muslims. From your talk you are polytheists." The three drivers are taken to the side road and there is gunfire as they are murdered.

The armed opposition in Syria and Iraq has become dominated by Salafi jihadists, fundamentalist Islamic fighters committed to holy war. Those killing non-Sunni drivers on the Damascus-Baghdad road are an all-too-typical example of this. Western governments may not care very much how many Shia die in Syria, Iraq, or Pakistan, but they can see that Sunni movements with beliefs similar to the al-Qaeda of Osama bin Laden have a base in Iraq and Syria today far larger than anything they enjoyed in Afghanistan before 9/11 when they were subordinate to the Taliban.

The pretense that the Western-backed and suppos-edly secular Free Syrian Army was leading the fight to overthrow President Bashar al-Assad finally evapo-rated in December 2013 as jihadists overran their supply depots and killed their commanders. Saudi Arabia was centrally involved in this ascendancy of jihadists in the opposition movement. It had taken over from Qatar as the main funder of the Syrian rebels in the summer of 2013. But Saudi involvement had been much deeper and more long-term than just increased funding, with more fighters coming to Syria from Saudi Arabia than from any other country.

Saudi preachers called vehemently for armed intervention against Assad, either by individual volunteers or by states. The beliefs of Wahhabism, the puritanical literalist Saudi version of Islam recognized exclusively by the Saudi educational and judicial system, are not much different from those of al-Qaeda or other Salafi jihadist groups across the Middle East. Wahhabism wholly rejects other types of Islamic worship as well as non-Muslim beliefs. It regards Shi'ism as a heresy, in much the same way Roman Catholics in Reformation Europe detested and sought to eliminate Protestantism.

There is no doubt that well-financed Wahhabi propaganda has contributed to the deepening and increasingly violent struggle between Sunni and Shia. A 2013 study published by the directorate-general for external policies of the European Parliament, called "The involvement of Salafism/Wahhabism in the support and supply of arms to rebel groups around the world," begins by saying:

"Saudi Arabia has been a major source of financing to rebel and terrorist organizations since the 1980s." It adds that Saudi Arabia has given $10 billion (£6 billion) to promote the Wahhabi agenda and predicts that the "number of indoctrinated jihadi fighters" will increase.

The origins of Saudi Arabia's anti-Shia stance can be traced back to the alliance between the Wahhabis and the House of Saud dating from the eighteenth century. But the key date for the development of the jihadist movements as political players is 1979, with the Soviet invasion of Afghanistan and the Iranian revolution, when Ayatollah Khomeini turned Iran into a Shia theocracy.

During the 1980s, an alliance was born among Saudi Arabia, Pakistan (or more properly the Pakistani army), and the US that has proved extraordinarily durable. It has been one of the main supports of American predominance in the region, but also provided a seed plot for jihadist movements, out of which Osama bin Laden's al-Qaeda was originally only one strain.

The shock of 9/11 provided a Pearl Harbor moment in the US when public revulsion and fear could be manipulated to implement a preexisting neo-conservative agenda by targeting Saddam Hussein and invading Iraq. A reason for waterboarding al-Qaeda suspects was to extract confessions implicating Iraq rather than Saudi Arabia in the attacks.

The 9/11 Commission report identified Saudi Arabia as the main source of al-Qaeda financing but no action was taken on the basis of it. Six years after the attack, at the height of the military conflict in Iraq in 2007, Stuart Levey, the under secretary of the US Treasury in charge of monitoring and impeding terror financing, told ABC News that, when it came to al-Qaeda, "If I could somehow snap my fingers and cut off the funding from one country, it would be Saudi Arabia." He added that not one person identified by the US or the UN as funding terrorism had been prosecuted by the Saudis.

Despite this high-level frustration at the Saudis for not cooperating, nothing much had improved a couple of years later. As previously mentioned, in a cable released by WikiLeaks in December 2009, US Secretary of State Hillary Clinton wrote: "Saudi Arabia remains a critical financial support base for al-Qaeda, the Taliban, LeT [Lashkar-e-Taiba in Pakistan] and other terrorist groups." She complained that insofar as Saudi Arabia did act against al-Qaeda, it was as a domestic threat and not against its activities abroad.

A further point that came across strongly in leaked American diplomatic traffic was the extent to which the

Saudis gave priority to confronting the Shia. Here the paranoia ran deep. Take Pakistan, Saudi Arabia's most important Muslim ally, of which a senior Saudi diplomat said that "we are not observers in Pakistan, we are participants." Pre-9/11, only Saudi Arabia, Pakistan, and the United Arab Emirates (UAE) had given official recognition to the Taliban as the government of Afghanistan.

There is something hysterical and exaggerated about Saudi fear of Shia expansionism, since the Shia are powerful only in the handful of countries where they are in the majority or are a strong minority. Of fifty-seven Muslim countries, just four have a Shia majority.

Nevertheless, the Saudis were highly suspicious of Pakistani President Asif Ali Zardari and made clear they would have much preferred a military dictatorship in Pakistan. The reason for the dislike was sectarian, according to UAE foreign minister Sheikh Abdullah bin Zayed, who told the Americans that "Saudi Arabia suspects that Zardari is Shia, thus creating Saudi concern of a Shia triangle in the region between Iran, the Maliki government in Iraq, and Pakistan under Zardari."

Sectarian hostility to the Shia as heretics is combined with fear and loathing of Iran. King Abdullah continuously urged America to attack Iran and "cut off the head of the snake." Rolling back the influence of the Shia majority in Iraq was another priority. Here was another reason why so many Saudis sympathized with the actions of jihadists in Iraq against the government.

The takeover of Iraq by a Shia government—the first in the Arab world since Saladin overthrew the Fatimid dynasty in Egypt in 1171—caused serious alarm in Riyadh and other Sunni capitals, whose rulers wanted to reverse this historic defeat. The Iraqi government noticed with alarm in 2009 that, when a Saudi imam issued a fatwa calling on the Shia to be killed, Sunni governments in the region were "suspiciously silent" when it came to condemning his statement.

The Arab uprisings of 2011 exacerbated sectarianism, including in Saudi Arabia, which is always highly conscious of the Shia minority in its Eastern Province. In March 2011, 1,500 Saudi troops provided backup for the al-Khalifa royal family in Bahrain as they crushed pro-democracy protests by the Shia majority on the island. The openly sectarian nature of the clampdown was made clear when Shia shrines were bulldozed.

In Syria, the Saudis underestimated the staying power of the Assad government and the support it was receiving from Russia, Iran, and Hezbollah in Lebanon. But Saudi involvement, along with that of Qatar and Turkey, de-emphasized secular democratic change as the ideology of the uprising, which then turned into a Sunni bid for power using Salafi jihadist brigades as the cutting edge of the revolt. Predictably, the Alawites and other minorities felt they had no choice but to fight to the death.

In the period that followed, there were signs of real anger in Washington at actions by Saudi Arabia and the Sunni monarchies of the Gulf in supplying and financing jihadi warlords in Syria. The US was increasingly fearful that such support would create a situation similar to that in Afghanistan in the 1980s, when indiscriminate backing for insurgents ultimately produced al-Qaeda, the Taliban, and jihadi warlords. The head of US intelligence, James Clapper, estimated the number of foreign fighters in Syria, mostly from the Arab world, at around 7,000.

US Secretary of State John Kerry privately criticized Prince Bandar bin Sultan, head of Saudi intelligence since 2012 and former Saudi ambassador in Washington, who had been masterminding the campaign to overthrow the Assad government. Prince Bandar struck back by denouncing President Obama for not intervening militarily in Syria when chemical weapons were used against civilians.

But it was clear that the Saudis too were concerned that jihadis whom they had previously allowed to leave to join the war in Syria might return home and turn their weapons against the rulers of the kingdom. During February and March 2014, in an abrupt reversal of previous policy, Saudi Arabia sought to stop Saudi fighters departing for Syria and called on all other foreign fighters to leave that country. King Abdullah decreed it a crime for Saudis to fight in foreign conflicts. The Saudi intelligence chief, Prince Bandar bin Sultan, who had been in charge of organizing, funding, and supplying jihadi groups, was unexpectedly removed from overseeing Saudi policy towards Syria, and was replaced by interior minister Mohammed bin Nayef, who had a better relationship with the US and was chiefly known for his campaign against al-Qaeda in the Arabian Peninsula.

Prince Miteb bin Abdullah, son of the Saudi King Abdullah and head of the Saudi National Guard, would also play a role in formulating a new Syrian policy. Saudi Arabia's differences with some of the other Gulf monarchies were becoming more explicit, with the Saudis, Bahrain, and the United Arab Emirates withdrawing their ambassadors from Qatar in March of 2014. This was primarily because of Qatar's backing for the Muslim Brotherhood in Egypt, but also for its funding and supplying of out-of-control jihadi groups in Syria.

By March 2014, US under secretary for terrorism and financial intelligence David Cohen was praising Saudi Arabia for progress in stamping out al-Qaeda funding sources within its own borders, but warning that other jihadist groups could still access donors in the kingdom. He also pointed out that Saudi Arabia was not alone among the Gulf monarchies in supporting jihadists, stating sourly that "our ally Kuwait has become the epicenter for fundraising for terrorist groups in Syria." He complained particularly about the appointment of Nayef al-Ajmi as both minister of justice and minister of Islamic endowments (Awqaf) and Islamic affairs, noting that: "Al-Ajmi has a history of promoting jihad in Syria. In fact, his image has been featured on fundraising posters for a prominent al-Nusra Front financier." Under US pressure, he was forced to resign.

It is likely to be too late for Saudi Arabia to manage a clear-cut reversal in its support for the jihadis in Syria. Jihadist social media is now openly attacking the Saudi royal family. A picture of King Abdullah giving a medal to President George W. Bush in earlier years is scathingly captioned: "Medal for invading two Islamic countries." Another more menacing photo on a Twitter account is taken in the back of a pickup truck. It shows armed and masked fighters and the caption reads: "With God's will we'll enter the Arabia Peninsula like this. Today the Levant and tomorrow al-Qurayat and Arrar [two cities in northern Saudi Arabia]."

Certainly, Shia leaders are doubtful that the Saudi U-turn is happening at a deep enough level. Yousif al-Khoei, who heads the Centre for Academic Shi'a Studies, says: "The recent Saudi fatwas de-legitimizing suicide killings is a positive step, but the Saudis need a serious attempt to reform their educational system which currently demonizes Shias, Sufis, Christians, Jews and other sects and religions. They need to stop the preaching of hate from so many satellite stations, and not allow a free ride for their preachers of hate on the social media."

Shia leaders cite a number of fatwas issued by Saudi clerics targeting them as non-Muslims. One such declares: "To call for closeness between Shia and Sunni is similar to closeness between Islam and Christianity."

Christian churches are considered by adherents of Wahhabism as places of idolatry and polytheism because of pictures of Jesus and his mother and the use of the cross, all of which show that Christians do not worship a single God. This is not a view confined to Saudi Arabia:

in Bahrain, seventy-one Sunni clerics demanded that the government withdraw its permission for a Christian church to be built. When the al-Khalifa royal family crushed pro-democracy protests by the Shia majority in Bahrain in 2011, the first act of the security forces was to destroy several dozen mosques, shrines, and graves of Shia holy men, on the grounds that they had not received the correct building permits.

The "Wahhabisation" of mainstream Sunni Islam is one of the most dangerous developments of our era. Ali Allawi, the historian and authority on sectarianism, says that in country after country, Sunni communities "have adopted tenets of Wahhabism that [were] not initially part of their canon." A crucial feature in the rise of Wahhabism is the financial and political might of Saudi Arabia. Dr. Allawi says that if, for example, a pious Muslim wants to found a seminary in Bangladesh, there are not many places he can obtain £20,000 other than from Saudi Arabia. But if the same person wants to oppose Wahhabism, then he will have "to fight with limited resources." The result is deepening sectarianism as Shia are targeted as non-Muslims, and non-Muslims of all descriptions are forced to flee, so that countries such as Iraq and Syria are being emptied of Christians who have lived there for almost 2,000 years.

Dr. Allawi says that it is naïve to imagine that small Shia minorities in countries such as Malaysia or Egypt were not frowned upon in the past by the majority Sunni, but it is only recently that they have been ostracized and persecuted. He says that many Shia now live with a sense of impending doom, "like Jews in Germany in 1935." As with European anti-Semitic propaganda down the ages, Shia are demonized for supposedly carrying out abominable practices such as ritual incest. In a village near Cairo in 2013, four Shia men were murdered by a mob while carrying out their usual religious ceremonies in a private house.

"The Wahhabi try to ignore the entire corpus of Islamic teaching over the last 1,400 years," says Dr. Allawi. The ideology of al-Qaeda–type movements in Iraq and Syria is not the same as Wahhabism. But their beliefs are similar, just carried to a greater extreme. There are bizarre debates about whether it is forbidden to clap or whether women should wear bras. As with Boko Haram in Nigeria, militants in Iraq and Syria see no religious prohibition in enslaving women as spoils of war.

There are signs that the Saudi rulers may now be coming to regret giving quite so much support to the jihadis trying to overthrow President Assad in Syria.

For instance, early in 2014 they invited the Iranian foreign minister to visit the kingdom. But it may be too late: having heard their government denounce Assad as the root of all evil in Syria, Saudi jihadis will see it as a betrayal and the height of hypocrisy if that same government now threatens them with prison terms when they return home.

8

If It Bleeds It Leads

The four wars fought in Afghanistan, Iraq, Libya, and Syria over the past twelve years have all involved overt or covert foreign intervention in deeply divided countries. In each case the involvement of the West exacerbated existing differences and pushed hostile parties towards civil war. In each country, all or part of the opposition has been hard-core jihadi fighters. Whatever the real issues at stake, the interventions have been presented by politicians as primarily humanitarian, in support of popular forces against dictators and police states. Despite apparent military successes, in none of these cases have the local opposition and their backers succeeded in consolidating power or establishing stable states.

But there is another similarity that connects the four conflicts: more than most armed struggles, they have all been propaganda wars in which newspaper, television, and radio journalists played a central role. In every war there is a difference between reported news and what really happened, but during these four campaigns the outside world has been left with misconceptions, even about the identity of the victors and the defeated.

In 2001, reports of the Afghan war gave the impression that the Taliban had been beaten decisively, even though there had been very little fighting. In 2003, there was a belief in the West that Saddam Hussein's forces had been crushed when in fact the Iraqi army, including the units of the elite Special Republican Guard, had simply disbanded and gone home. In Libya in 2011, the rebel militiamen, so often shown on television firing truck-mounted heavy machine guns in the general direction of the enemy, had only a limited role in the overthrow of Muammar Gaddafi, who was mostly brought down by NATO air strikes. In Syria in 2011 and 2012, foreign leaders and journalists repeatedly and vainly predicted the imminent defeat of Bashar al-Assad.

These misperceptions explain why there have been

so many surprises and unexpected reversals of fortune. The Taliban rose again in 2006 because it hadn't been beaten as comprehensively as the rest of the world imagined. At the end of 2001, I was able to drive, nervously but safely, from Kabul to Kandahar. But when I tried to make the same journey in 2011, I could go no farther south on the main road than the last police station on the outskirts of Kabul. In Tripoli two years ago, hotels were filled to capacity with journalists covering Gaddafi's fall and the triumph of the rebel militias. But state authority still hasn't been restored there. In the summer of 2013, Libya almost stopped exporting oil because the main ports on the Mediterranean had been seized as a result of a mutiny among militiamen. The prime minister, Ali Zeidan, threatened to bomb "from the air and the sea" the oil tankers the militiamen were using to sell oil on the black market. Soon Zeidan himself was forced to flee the country.

Libya's descent into anarchy was scarcely covered by the international media. They had long since moved on to Syria, and more recently to Egypt. Iraq, home a few years ago to so many foreign news bureaus, has also dropped off the media map, although up to a thousand Iraqis are killed each month, mostly as a result of the bombing of civilian targets. When it rained for a few days in Baghdad in January, the sewer system, supposedly restored at a cost of $7 billion, couldn't cope: some streets were knee-deep in dirty water and sewage. In Syria, many opposition fighters who had fought heroically to defend their communities turned into licensed bandits and racketeers when they took power in rebel-held enclaves.

It wasn't that reporters were factually incorrect in their descriptions of what they had seen. But the very term "war reporter," though not often used by journalists themselves, helps explain what went wrong. Leaving aside its macho overtones, it gives the misleading impression that war can be adequately described by focusing on military combat. Irregular or guerrilla wars are always intensely political, and none more so than the strange stop-and-go conflicts that followed from 9/11. This doesn't mean that what happened on the battlefield was insignificant, but only that it requires interpretation. In 2003, television showed columns of Iraqi tanks smashed and on fire after US air strikes on the main highway north of Baghdad. If it hadn't been for the desert background, viewers could have been watching pictures of the defeated German army in Normandy in 1944. But I climbed into some of the tanks and could see that they had been abandoned long before they were hit. This

but not enough to prevent counterrevolution, as the military coup in Egypt on July 3, 2013, underscored. The initial success of street demonstrations led to over-confidence and excessive reliance on spontaneous action; the need for leadership, organization, unity, and policies that amounted to more than a vague humanitarian agenda all went by the wayside. History, including the histories of their own countries, had little to teach this generation of radicals and would-be revolutionaries. They drew no lessons from what had happened when Nasser seized power in Egypt in 1952, and didn't ask whether the Arab uprisings of 2011 might have parallels with the European revolutions of 1848, easy victories that were swiftly reversed. Many members of the intelligentsia in Libya and Syria seemed to live and think within the echo chamber of the Internet. Few expressed practical ideas about the way forward.

Conviction that a toxic government is the root of all evil is the public position of most oppositions, but it is dangerous to trust one's own propaganda. The Iraqi opposition genuinely believed that Iraq's sectarian and ethnic problems stemmed from Saddam and that once he was gone all would be well. The opposition in Libya and Syria believed that the regimes of Gaddafi and Assad were so demonstrably bad that it was counterrevolutionary to question whether what came after them would be better. Foreign reporters have by and large shared these opinions. I recall mentioning some of the failings of the Libyan militiamen to a Western journalist: "Just remember who the good guys are," she replied reprovingly.

Good guys they may have been, but there was something troubling about the ease with which oppositionists provided media-friendly locations, whether in Tahrir Square or at the frontlines in Libya. Protesters in Benghazi would hold up placards written in perfect English, which they often could not read themselves, for the benefit of television viewers. At Ajdabiya, two hours' drive along the main coast road south of Benghazi, foreign journalists often outnumbered opposition fighters, and cameramen had to maneuver their correspondents so the predominance of the press wasn't evident to their audience. The main danger there was being run over by a pickup truck fitted with a heavy machine gun: the drivers often panicked when a shell exploded in the distance. The Libyan militiamen were effective when they were fighting for their own cities and towns, but without an air umbrella they wouldn't have lasted more than a few weeks. Media focus on colorful skirmishes diverted attention from the central fact that

Gaddafi was overthrown by military intervention on the part of the US, Britain, and France.

There is nothing surprising about all this. Public appearances by Western leaders with smiling children or cheering soldiers are invariably contrived to show them in a sympathetic light. Why shouldn't Arab rebels have the same public relations skills? The problem was the way war reporters so quickly accepted and publicized opposition atrocity stories. In Libya one of the most influential stories described the mass rape of women in rebel areas by government troops acting on orders from above. A Libyan psychologist claimed to have distributed seventy thousand questionnaires in rebel-controlled areas, out of which sixty thousand were returned. Some 259 women volunteered that they had been raped; the psychologist said she had interviewed 140 of them. That such precise statistics could have been collected in the anarchy of eastern Libya was implausible, but her story was uncritically repeated, doing much to turn Gaddafi into a pariah. Largely ignored were reports a few weeks later from Amnesty International, Human Rights Watch, and a UN commission saying that there was no evidence for the story, which appears to have been nothing more than a highly successful propaganda ploy. On another occasion, the rebels showed off the bodies of eight government soldiers: they claimed the men had been executed by their own side for trying to defect to the opposition. Later, Amnesty International unearthed a video showing the eight men alive after being captured by the rebels; clearly, they had been killed soon afterwards and their deaths blamed on pro-Gaddafi forces.

The essential ingredients of a good atrocity story are that it should be shocking and not immediately refutable. In 1990, it was widely reported that Kuwaiti babies had been tipped from their hospital incubators by invading Iraqi soldiers and left to die on the floor. Immensely influential at the time, the story was only discredited when the person who claimed to have witnessed it turned out to be the daughter of the Kuwaiti ambassador to Washington; she had not been in the hospital at the time. Reporters may have their suspicions, but they can seldom disprove such tales straightaway. They also know that news editors don't welcome being told that a colorful news story, which their competitors will very likely run, is probably false. It's easy to put the blame on the "fog of war" and it's true that fighting involves confusing and fast-moving events, reports of which can't be checked. Everybody in a war has a more-than-usual strong motive for misrepresenting their achievements and failures, and it's usually difficult to disprove their claims. This is scarcely new. "Did it ever occur to you, sir, what an opportunity a battlefield affords liars?" the Confederate general Stonewall Jackson once remarked to an aide.

When people are shooting at one another, it is, of course, often dangerous to hang around long enough to establish what's really going on. In Syria in June 2014, I was interviewing the governor of Homs when he unexpectedly claimed that the Syrian army had taken over a town on the Lebanese border called Tal Kalakh, previously held by the opposition. He suggested I go there to see for myself. The opposition was saying that fierce fighting was continuing and al-Jazeera reported that smoke was rising from the town. I spent three hours driving around Tal Kalakh, which was certainly under full government control, and didn't hear a shot fired or see any smoke. Part of the town had been badly damaged by shelling and the streets were empty—though a government sympathizer claimed this was because "people are taking their siesta."

While in Damascus I stayed in the Christian district of Bab Touma, which was being hit by mortar bombs fired from rebel-held districts. A friend rang to say that four people had been killed by a suicide bomber a few hundred yards away. I went there at once and saw a body under a white sheet; on the other side of the street was a small crater that looked as if it had been made by an exploding mortar round. Syrian state television kept claiming that the dead man was a suicide bomber who had been targeting a Christian church; they even named him. For once, it was possible to know exactly what had happened: CCTV footage taken from the street showed a falling mortar bomb outlined for an instant against the white shirt of a passerby. He was killed instantly and wrongly identified as the bomber. Syrian TV later apologized for its mistake.

In each of these cases, political bias and simple error combined to produce a misleading version of events, but it had little to do with the "fog of war." All it really establishes is that there is no alternative to first-hand reporting. Journalists rarely fully admit to themselves or others the degree to which they rely on secondary and self-interested sources. The problem is compounded because people caught up in newsworthy events often convince themselves that they know more than they do. Survivors of suicide bombings in Baghdad would describe to me in minute detail the bomber's facial expression moments before he detonated his explosives, forgetting that if they had been that close they would be dead. The best witnesses were small boys selling cigarettes, who were always on the lookout for customers.

In reality, war isn't much foggier than peace, sometimes less so. Serious developments are difficult to hide because thousands are affected by them. And once the fighting has started, the authorities become increasingly less able to monitor and impede an enterprising journalist's movements. Secrets about who holds what territory and who is winning and losing become difficult to keep. Informants become easier to find. In times of danger, whether in Belfast, Basra, or Damascus, people become acutely aware of any potential threat to their neighborhood: it can be as small as a new face or as large as the arrival of a military unit. A government or an army can try to maintain secrecy by banning reporters but they will pay the price as the vacuum of news is filled with information supplied by their enemies. The Syrian government put itself at a political disadvantage by denying visas to most foreign journalists, a policy it has only recently begun to reverse.

As the danger increased in Iraq after 2003, a rumor spread that foreign reporters weren't really eyewitnesses because they had been reduced to producing "hotel journalism," never leaving three or four well-fortified hotels. This was never true, quite apart from the fact that these hotels were repeatedly targeted by suicide bombers. Journalists who were frightened of leaving their hotels took the sensible precaution of not going to Baghdad in the first place. I used to think that the reporters most likely to be killed or kidnapped were the inexperienced ones who were trying to make a name for themselves by taking outrageous risks. But the war reporters I knew best who died, such as David Blundy in El Salvador in 1989 and Marie Colvin in Syria in 2012, were highly experienced. Their only mistake was to go to dangerous places so frequently that there was a high chance that they would one day be hit by a bullet or a bomb.

Messy guerrilla fighting and sporadic artillery bombardments in wars with no clear frontlines are particularly dangerous. In 2004, I was nearly killed outside Kufa on the Euphrates by Shia militiamen who had been rattled by fighting with US marines earlier in the day. Suspicious of the local headdress I was wearing, they half-decided I was a spy. But I had put on the headdress as a basic disguise, in order to travel through Sunni-held villages on the road between Kufa and Baghdad.

The idea that foreign journalists just lurk in their hotels in Damascus, Baghdad, or Kabul is absurd. A more substantive charge is that they write too much about firefights and skirmishes, the fireworks of war, while neglecting the broader picture that might determine the outcome. "My newspaper doesn't do what it calls 'bang-bang' journalism," one correspondent said grandly, explaining why none of his colleagues was covering the fighting in Syria first-hand. But the "bang-bang" matters: war may not be explicable without the politics, but the politics can't be understood without the war. Early on in the occupation of Iraq, I went to al-Dohra power station in Baghdad after one American soldier was shot dead there and another wounded. This was a minor incident in an incipient guerrilla war, but the approval of local people as they stood around the pool of dried blood on the pavement was significant. "We are very poor but we will celebrate by cooking a chicken," one man said. "God willing, there will be more actions like this."

Embedding with the American and British armies meant that the journalists ended up having the same experiences as the soldiers and thinking many of the same thoughts. It's difficult not to bond with people who are important to one's safety and with whom one shares common dangers. Armies prefer the embedding system in part because they can favor sympathetic reporters and exclude the more critical ones. For journalists, counter-intuitively, it often means missing crucial parts of a war, since an experienced guerrilla commander will naturally attack wherever the enemy forces are absent or weak. Anybody embedded with the army will tend to be in the wrong place at the wrong time. In 2004, when the US marines stormed the city of Fallujah, killing many insurgents, they were accompanied by most of Baghdad's press corps. It was a famous and well-publicized victory. But the insurgent counterstrike, the capture of the much larger city of Mosul in northern Iraq, from which US soldiers had withdrawn, was largely ignored by the media at the time. When Mosul fell a second time in June 2014, few commentators even mentioned that the city had been take over by insurgents ten years earlier, or took on board the implication of this, which was that Baghdad's control of its second city and the main stronghold of the urban Sunni had always been shaky.

The most sinister change in the way war is perceived through the media springs from what just a few years ago seemed to be a wholly positive development. Satellite television and the use of information supplied by YouTube, bloggers, and social media were portrayed as liberating innovations at the beginning of the Arab Spring. The monopoly on information imposed by police states from Tunisia to Egypt and Bahrain had been broken. But as the course of the uprising in Syria has shown, satellite television and the Internet can also be used to spread propaganda and hate.

"Half of Jihad is Media" is one slogan posted on a jihadist website, which, taken broadly, is wholly correct. The ideas, actions, and aims of fundamentalist Sunni jihadists are broadcast daily through satellite television stations, YouTube, Twitter, and Facebook. As long as such powerful means of propagandizing exist, groups similar to al-Qaeda will never go short of money or recruits.

Much of what is disseminated by the jihadists is hate propaganda against Shia and, more occasionally, against Christians, Sufis, and Jews. It calls for support for jihad in Syria, Iraq, Yemen, and anywhere else holy war is being waged. A recent posting shows a romantic-looking suicide bomber who was "martyred" carrying out an attack on an Egyptian police station in Sinai.

Looking at a selection of such online postings, what is striking is not only their violence and sectarianism but also the professionalism with which they are produced. The jihadists may yearn for a return to the norms of early Islam, but their skills in using modern communications and the Internet are well ahead of most political movements in the world. By producing a visual record of everything it does, ISIS has greatly amplified its political impact. Its militants dominate social media and produce well-made and terrifying films to illustrate the commitment of their fighters as they identify and kill their enemies. The Iraqi government approach to media differs radically: attempting to maintain morale by downplaying ISIS successes, emphasizing patriotism, and stressing that Baghdad can never fall. Crude propaganda like this frequently leads viewers to switch to al-Arabiya, based in Dubai but Saudi owned, or other channels that broadcast images of the events unfolding across the country, giving the advantage to ISIS propaganda.

In contrast to the sophistication of the technical production of footage by militants, the content is frequently crudely sectarian and violent. Take for instance three pictures from Iraq. The first shows two men in uniform, their hands tied behind their backs, lying dead on what looks like a cement floor. Blood flows from their heads as if they have been shot or their throats cut. The caption reads: "Shia have no medicine but the sword—Anbar victories."

The second picture shows two armed men beside two bodies, identified by the caption as members of the anti-al-Qaeda Sunni Awakening movement in Iraq's Salah

ad-Din province. The third shows a group of Iraqi soldiers holding a regimental banner, but the words on it
have been changed to make them offensive to Sunni: "God
curse Omar and Abu Bakr" (two early Sunni leaders).

Such Internet postings often include appeals for
money, issued by Sunni clergy and politicians, to finance
jihadi fighters. One such appeal claimed to have raised
$2,500 (£1,500) for each of the 12,000 fighters that the
group responsible for the appeal had sent to Syria.
Another included a picture showing seven shelves, as
if in a retail store, which, on closer inspection, could
each be seen as displaying a different kind of grenade.
The caption beneath the photograph read: "Anbar's
mujahedeen pharmacy for Shia." ISIS images have also
appeared showing prisoners being loaded into flatbed
trucks by masked gunmen and later forced to lie face
down in a shallow ditch with their arms tied behind
their backs. Final pictures showed the blood-covered
bodies of captive soldiers, probably Shia, who made up
much of the rank-and-file of the Iraqi army. Captions
indicated the massacre was in revenge for the death of
an ISIS commander, Abdul-Rahman al-Beilawy, whose
killing was reported just before ISIS' surprise offensive
that swept through northern Iraq, capturing the Sunni
strongholds of Mosul and Tikrit, in mid-June 2014.

It is not just Twitter and Facebook accounts that are used by the jihadists. Two television stations based in Egypt (but reportedly financed from Saudi Arabia and Kuwait), Safa and Wesal, employ journalists and commentators who are vocally hostile to the Shia. Wesal TV broadcasts in five languages: Arabic, Farsi, Kurdish, Indonesian, and Hausa. The Iraqi government response has been to close down some "enemy television stations" as well as Facebook, YouTube, Twitter, and other Internet services, although Iraqis are quick to find ways around official censorship. Followers of ISIS continually flood Twitter with pictures of the bodies of their enemies, but they also use the medium to show functioning hospitals and a consultative administrative process.

Hate preachers, likewise, can incite large numbers of followers on YouTube. Sheikh Mohammad al-Zughbi, a popular vlogger in Egypt, calls on God to protect Egypt from "the criminal traitors and the criminal Shia," as well as from the Jews and Crusaders. Another sermon entitled "Oh Syria, the victory is coming" says President Assad is "seeking help from these Persians, the Shia, the traitors, the Shia criminals."

Such rants could be dismissed as being addressed to a small, fanatical audience, but the numbers of viewers show them to be immensely popular. Observers of the rebels in Syria have noted how much time they spend on the Internet, using it to follow what they believe is happening elsewhere in the conflict. Further evidence about the impact of satellite television and jihadist websites comes from prisoners taken in Iraq. While, like all prisoners, they are inclined to say what their captors want to hear, their accounts in interviews on Iraqi television ring true. Waleed bin Muhammad al-Hadi al-Masmoudi from Tunisia, the third-largest supplier of foreign jihadists to Syria, told one such program that in making his decision to come to Iraq to fight he "was deeply influenced by al-Jazeera TV channel." Together with thirteen other volunteers from Saudi Arabia, Jordan, and Yemen, he had no difficulty in making his way to Fallujah. In another interview, Abdullah Azam Salih al-Qahtani, a former Saudi officer, said: "Arabic media and jihadist websites convinced me to come."

Some of the portrayals of atrocities that appear on computers and television screens across the world, supposedly within hours of having taken place, are fraudulent. ISIS successes in Iraq are sometimes fabricated with the footage used to advertise them taken in Syria or Libya, or even outside the Middle East altogether. A correspondent in southeast Turkey recently visited a Syrian refugee camp where he found ten-year-old children watching a YouTube clip of two men being executed with a chainsaw. The commentary claimed that the victims were Syrian Sunnis and the killers were Alawites; in fact the film was from Mexico and the murders had been carried out by a drug lord to intimidate his rivals.

Such fraudulent atrocity stories have an effect on a war: a Libyan militiaman who believes that the government soldiers he is fighting are under orders to rape his wife and daughters isn't going to take many prisoners. But more often the pictures of murder and torture are accurate. Their rapid dissemination explains the ferocity of the conflict in Syria and the difficulty the participants have in negotiating an end to their civil war.

The Arab Spring revolts were a strange mixture of revolution, counterrevolution, and foreign intervention. The international media often became highly confused about what was going on. The revolutionaries of 2011 had many failings but they were highly skilled in influencing and manipulating press coverage. Tahrir Square in Cairo and later the Maidan in Kiev became the arenas where a melodrama pitting the forces of good against evil was played out in front of the television cameras. Good reporters still took immense risks, and sometimes paid with their lives, trying to explain that there was more to what was happening than this oversimplified picture. But the worst media coverage, particularly in the first two years of the revolts, was very bad indeed. One correspondent remarked caustically that trying to describe post-2011 events in Syria from Beirut while relying on rebel sources was "like reporting the last American presidential election from Canada depending on members of the Tea Party faction of the Republican Party for information."

Predictably, such news was so biased and unreliable that the real course of events turned out to be full of unexpected developments and nasty surprises. This is likely to continue.

9

Shock and War

In the second half of 2013 I started to write about the way in which jihadis were taking over the Syrian armed opposition; at the same time there was mounting evidence that ISIS, formerly al-Qaeda in Iraq, was rapidly increasing in strength. My newspaper, the *Independent*, asked me to nominate a "man of the year" for the Middle East and I chose Abu Bakr al-Baghdadi, the shadowy figure who had become leader of ISIS in 2010. A few days later, on January 3, 2014, ISIS moved into Fallujah and the government proved unable to recapture it. This was not quite as alarming as it might have been because the Iraqi prime minister was emphasizing the mortal threat posed by Sunni counterrevolution in Anbar province to scare the Shia majority into voting for him in the parliamentary election on April 30 as "Mr. Security" and forgetting about government corruption and the lack of services. I thought that perhaps the failure to recapture the city was a deliberate electoral ploy and the assault on it would come after the poll.

But then well-informed Iraqis told me that the failure to retake Fallujah and crush ISIS in Anbar and elsewhere in northern Iraq had not happened for lack of trying. Five of the fifteen divisions in the Iraqi army had been deployed in Anbar and had suffered heavy losses from casualties and desertions. Soldiers were sent to the front with only four clips of ammunition for their AK-47s; they went hungry because their commanders had embezzled the money to be spent on food; in oil-rich Iraq, fuel for army vehicles was in short supply; some battalions were down to a quarter of their established strength. "The army has suffered a very bad defeat in Anbar," a former Iraqi minister told me sometime in April.

Despite these warnings, I was shocked a month or so later when, on June 10, Mosul fell almost without a fight. Every derogatory story I had ever heard about the Iraqi army being a financial racket in which commanders bought their posts in order to grow rich on kickbacks and embezzlement turned out to be true. The ordinary soldiers may have run away in Mosul but not as quickly as their generals, who turned up in civilian clothes in Erbil, the Kurdish capital. It had become apparent over the previous year that ISIS was run with a chilling blend of ideological fanaticism and military efficiency. Its campaign to take northern and western Iraq was expertly planned, choosing soft targets and avoiding well defended positions, or, as ISIS put it, moving "like a serpent through rocks."

It was evident that Western governments had entirely misread the situation in Iraq and Syria. For two years Iraqi politicians had been warning anybody who would listen to them that if the civil war in Syria continued it would destabilize the fragile status quo in Iraq. When Mosul fell everybody blamed Maliki, who certainly had a lot to answer for, but the real cause of the debacle in Iraq was the war across Iraq's border. The revolt of the Syrian Sunni had caused a similar explosion in Iraq. Maliki had treated the Sunni provinces like a conquered country, but the Iraqi Sunni would not have risen again without the example and encouragement of their Syrian counterparts. The ascendancy of ISIS that resulted from its being able to act as the shock troops of a general Sunni revolt may yet be reversible. But the offensive they led in the summer of 2014 has likely ended forever the Shia-dominated state that was brought into being by the American invasion of 2003.

The fall of Mosul was only the latest of a series of unpleasant and unexpected events in the Middle East to catch the outside world by surprise. The region has always been treacherous ground for foreign intervention, but many of the reasons for Western failure to read the situation in the Middle East are recent and self-inflicted. The US response to the attacks of 9/11 in 2001 targeted the wrong countries when Afghanistan and Iraq were identified as the hostile states whose governments needed to be overthrown. Meanwhile, the two countries most involved in supporting al-Qaeda and favoring the ideology behind the attacks, Saudi Arabia and Pakistan, were largely ignored and given a free pass. Both were long-standing US allies, and remained so despite 9/11. Saudi Arabia may be now pulling back on its sponsorship of jihadi fighters in Syria and elsewhere around the world for fear of blowback in the kingdom itself. Pakistan Prime Minister Nawaz Sharif may insist that he is doing all he can to rid the Pakistan security services of their extremist elements. But until the United States and its allies in the West recognize that these states are key in promoting Islamic extremism, little real progress will be made in the battle to isolate the jihadists.

It was not governments alone that got it wrong. So too did the reformers and revolutionaries who regarded the uprisings of the "Arab Spring" of 2011 as a death blow to the old authoritarian regimes across the region. For a brief moment, sectarianism and dictatorship seemed to be crumbling; the Arab world was standing at the entrance to a brave new future free of religious hate, where political enemies fought out their differences in democratic elections. Three years later, with the democracy movements having retreated all over the region in the face of successful counterrevolution and mounting sectarian violence, this enthusiasm seems naïve. It is worth analyzing why a progressive revolutionary alternative to police states and jihadi movements like ISIS has failed so comprehensively.

The revolutions and popular uprisings of 2011 were as genuine as any in history, but the way they were perceived, particularly in the West, was often seriously awry. Unexpectedness is in the nature of revolutionary change: I have always believed that if I can spot a revolution coming, so can the head of the Mukhabarat security police. He will do everything possible to prevent it happening. Real revolutions come into being because of an unpredictable and surprising coincidence of people and events with different motives coming together to target a common enemy such as Hosni Mubarak or Bashar al-Assad. The political, social, and economic roots of the upsurges of 2011 are very complex. That this wasn't obvious to everyone at the time is partly a result of the way foreign commentators exaggerated the role of new information technology. Protestors, skilled in propaganda if nothing else, saw the advantage of presenting the uprisings as unthreatening, "velvet" revolutions with English-speaking, well-educated bloggers and tweeters prominently in the vanguard. The purpose was to convey to Western publics that the new revolutionaries were comfortingly similar to themselves, and that what was happening in the Middle East in 2011 was like the anticommunist and pro-Western uprisings in Eastern Europe after 1989.

Opposition demands were all about personal freedom: social and economic inequalities were rarely declared to be issues, even when they were driving popular rage against the status quo. In the years prior to the Syrian revolt, the center of Damascus had been taken over by smart shops and restaurants, while the mass of Syrians saw their salaries stagnating in the face of rising prices. Farmers, ruined by four years of drought, were moving into shanty towns on the outskirts of the cities. The UN reported that between two and three million Syrians were living in "extreme poverty." Small manufacturing companies were being put out of business by cheap imports from Turkey and China. Economic liberalization, lauded in foreign capitals, was rapidly concentrating wealth in the hands of a politically well-connected few. Even members of the Mukhabarat, the secret police, were trying to survive on $200 a month. An International Crisis Group report pointed out that Syria's ruling class "has inherited power rather than fought for it ... and mimicked the ways of the urban upper class." The same was true of the quasi-monarchical families and their associates operating in parallel fashion in Egypt, Libya, and Iraq. Confident of their police-state protection, they ignored the hardships of the rest of the population, especially the underemployed, overeducated, and numerous youth, few of whom felt that they had any chance of improving their lives.

A simple-minded delusion that most problems would vanish once democracies had replaced the old police states was at the heart of the new reformist governments in the Middle East, be they in Iraq in 2005 or Libya in 2011. Opposition movements, persecuted at home or living a hand-to-mouth existence in exile, were reassured by such a notion and it was certainly easy to sell to foreign sponsors. However, a great disadvantage of this way of seeing things was that Saddam, Assad, and Gaddafi were so demonized it became difficult to engineer anything approaching a compromise or a peaceful transition from the old to a new regime. In Iraq in 2003 former members of the Baath Party were sacked, thus impoverishing a large part of the population, which had no alternative but to fight. The Syrian opposition refused to attend peace talks in Geneva in 2014 if Assad was allowed to play a role there, even though the areas of Syria under his control were home to most of the population. These exclusion policies were partly a way of guaranteeing jobs for the boys among the opposition. But they deepened sectarian, ethnic, and tribal divisions and provided the ingredients for civil war.

What is the glue that is supposed to hold these new post-revolutionary states together? Nationalism isn't much in favor in the West, where it is seen as a mask for racism or militarism, supposedly outmoded in an era of globalization and humanitarian intervention. But intervention in Iraq in 2003 and Libya in 2011 turned out to be very similar to imperial takeovers in the ninteenth century. There was absurd talk of "nation-building" to be carried out or assisted by foreign powers, which clearly had their own interests in mind just as Britain did when Lloyd George orchestrated the carve-up of the Ottoman Empire. A justification for the Arab leaders who seized power in the late 1960s was that they would create powerful states capable, finally, of giving reality to national independence. They didn't wholly fail: Gaddafi played a crucial role in raising the price of oil in 1973, and Hafez al-Assad, Bashar's father, who had taken power in Syria two years earlier, created a state that could hold its own in a protracted struggle with Israel for predominance in Lebanon. To opponents of these regimes, nationalism was simply a propaganda ploy on the part of ruthless dictatorships concerned to justify their hold on power. But without nationalism—even where the unity of the nation is something of a historic fiction—states lack an ideology that enables them to compete as a focus of loyalty with religious sects or ethnic groups.

It's easy enough to criticize the rebels and reformers in the Arab world for failing to resolve the dilemmas they faced in overturning the status quo. Their actions seem confused and ineffective when compared to the Cuban revolution or the liberation struggle in Vietnam. But the political terrain in which they have had to operate over the last twenty years has been particularly tricky. The dissolution of the Soviet Union in 1991 meant that the endorsement or tolerance of the US, and the US alone, was crucial for a successful takeover of power. Nasser was able to turn to Moscow to assert Egyptian independence in the Suez crisis of 1956, but after the Soviet collapse smaller states could no longer find a place for themselves between Moscow and Washington. Saddam said in 1990 that one of the reasons he invaded Kuwait when he did was that in the future such a venture would no longer be feasible as Iraq would be faced with unopposed American power. In the event, he got his diplomatic calculations spectacularly wrong, but his forecast was otherwise realistic, at least until perceptions of American military might were downgraded by Washington's failure to achieve its aims in Afghanistan and Iraq.

The deteriorating situation in Iraq and Syria may now have gone too far to re-create genuinely unitary states. Iraq is breaking up. Having taken over the northern oil city of Kirkuk, which they have long claimed as their capital, the Kurds will never surrender it or other disputed territories from which they were ethnically cleansed. Meanwhile, government rule over the Sunni Arab heartlands of north and central Iraq has evaporated with the disintegration of the Iraqi army. The government might continue to hold the capital and the Shia-majority provinces farther south, but it will have great difficulty in re-establishing its authority over Sunni villages and towns across the country. Dr. Safa Rusoul Hussein, the Iraqi deputy national security advisor, told me that "when 100 ISIS fighters take over an area they normally recruit five or ten times their original force. These are not frontline fighters and they may join just to defend their families, but ISIS numbers grow rapidly."

Outside help for the Iraqi government is unpredictable. Foreign intervention is as likely to come from Iran as from the United States. As a fellow Shia-majority state, Iraq matters even more to Tehran than Syria and Iran has emerged as the most influential foreign power in Baghdad since the 2003 invasion. The Iranian president Hassan Rouhani has said that Iran will act to combat "the violence and terrorism" of ISIS; indeed for a week the Baghdad rumor machine was claiming that Iranian battalions were already in Iraq, though this was unconfirmed by actual sightings. As for the US, war weariness at home rules out the return of ground troops, though advisers are being sent. Even air strikes are problematically effective because ISIS operates as a guerrilla army without easily visible movements of personnel or equipment that can be targeted. Its leadership is well practiced at keeping out of sight. The ISIS offensive has succeeded because it has been joined by a wide uprising of former Iraqi army officers who fought the Americans and young men from Sunni villages and towns across the country. Attacking such forces with manned aircraft or drones will further anger the Sunni community, and, if ISIS fighters start being killed by US airstrikes, it may not be long before an organization renowned for its ruthlessness when seeking revenge sends its suicide bombers to destroy American targets. In any event, the likelihood of US military success is remote. It's important to recall that, with air bases throughout the country and 150,000 soldiers on the ground, neither of which it has today, the US still failed to win an eight-year-long war.

Furthermore, the US is unlikely to want to appear as the preserver of Shia dominance over the Sunni minority, especially when exercised by a government in Baghdad that is as sectarian, corrupt, and dysfunctional as Saddam's ever was. There may be less state violence than before 2003, but only because the state is weaker. The Maliki government's methods are equally brutal: Iraqi prisons are full of people who have made false confessions under torture or the threat of it. Sunni villages near Fallujah are full of families with sons on death row. An Iraqi intellectual who had planned to open a museum in Abu Ghraib prison so that Iraqis would never forget the barbarities of Saddam's regime found that there was no space available because the cells were full of new inmates. Iraq is still an extraordinarily dangerous place. "I never imagined that ten years after the fall of Saddam you would still be able to get a man killed in Baghdad by paying $100," an Iraqi who'd been involved in the abortive museum project told me.

As Iraq disintegrates into separate Shia, Sunni, and Kurdish regions, the process is likely to be painful and violent. Sectarian confrontations will be unavoidable where there are mixed populations, such as in and around Baghdad with its seven million people. It seems unlikely that the country could be partitioned without extensive bloodshed and several million refugees. A possible outcome is an Iraqi version of the wrenching violence that accompanied the partition of India in 1947.

The situation is equally bleak in Syria. Too many conflicts and too many players have become involved for any peace terms to be acceptable to all. Comparison is frequently made with the Lebanese civil war, which lasted from 1975 to 1990, with the comforting moral drawn that, bloody though that conflict was, all sides eventually became exhausted and put away their guns. But the war did not quite end like that: it was Saddam Hussein's invasion of Kuwait in 1990 and Syria's decision to join the US-led coalition to evict him that led Washington to tolerate Syria extinguishing the last resistance to its rule in Lebanon. It is not a very comforting parallel.

There is no doubt that the Syrian people, both inside and outside the country, are utterly exhausted and demoralized by the civil war and would do almost anything to end it. But they are no longer in a position to determine their own fate. Saudi Arabia and Qatar are arming and training a new "moderate military opposition" that will supposedly fight Assad and ISIS and other al-Qaeda–type groups. But it is not clear that the "moderate" military opposition has any substance except as a tightly controlled cat's paw of foreign powers.

Only time will tell if President Assad is strong enough to break the current stalemate in Syria, though this seems unlikely. The combat forces of the Syrian army have hitherto been able to fight on only one front at a time, while it has become increasingly obvious that al-Qaeda–type movements, notably ISIS, JAN, and Ahrar al-Sham, can operate freely across Syria's borders with Iraq and Turkey. They have a vast hinterland in which to maneuver.

So long as the civil war continues, fanatical groups such as ISIS, with legions of fighters who are prepared to sacrifice their lives, will continue to hold the upper hand over moderates who might be more open to negotiations. In this situation, the importance of Syrian public opinion is diminishing steadily. However, it still counts for something. One of the few positive events to occur in Syria in the early summer of 2014 was the evacuation of the Old City of Homs by 1,200 fighters, who were allowed to bring their personal weapons to rebel-held territory, while, at the same time, two pro-regime Shia towns, Zahraa and Nubl, besieged for two years by the opposition, were able to receive humanitarian convoys. In addition, seventy hostages taken in Aleppo and Latakia were released. Encouragement can be drawn from the fact that different rebel groups were sufficiently coherent to negotiate and implement an agreement, something that had been deemed impossible. This kind of local peace negotiation cannot stop the overall conflict, but it can save lives along the way.

None of the religious parties that took power, whether in Iraq in 2005 or Egypt in 2012, has been able to consolidate its authority. Rebels everywhere look for support from the foreign enemies of the state they are trying to overthrow. The Syrian opposition can only reflect the policies and divisions of its sponsors. Resistance to the state was too rapidly militarized for opposition movements to develop an experienced national leadership and a political program. The discrediting of nationalism and communism, combined with the need to say what the US wanted to hear, meant that they were at the mercy of events, lacking any vision of a nonauthoritarian nation-state capable of competing with the religious fanaticism of the Sunni militants of ISIS and similar movements financed by the oil states of the Gulf. Now the results of this have spread across the border to Iraq. The Middle East is entering a long period of ferment in which counterrevolution may prove as difficult to consolidate as revolution itself.

Afterword

The long siege of the Syrian Kurdish town of Kobani by ISIS, ongoing at the time of writing, was the first serious check to the jihadis' advance. Over four months, they had won a succession of victories. In swift campaigns over the summer ISIS defeated the Iraqi army, the Syrian army, the Syrian rebels, and the Iraqi Kurdish peshmerga; it established a state stretching from Baghdad to Aleppo and from Syria's border with Turkey to the western deserts of Iraq.

Ethnic and religious groups of which the world had never heard or knew little, such as the Yazidis of Sinjar and the Chaldean Christians of Mosul, had become victims of ISIS's cruelty and sectarian bigotry. In September, it was the turn of the two-and-a-half million Syrian Kurds, who had gained de facto autonomy in three cantons in northern Syria just south of the Turkish border. One of these cantons, centered on the town of Kobani, became the target of a determined assault. By October 6, ISIS fighters had fought their way into the center of the town and its imminent fall was predicted by Turkish President Recep Tayyip Erdoğan, while US Secretary of State John Kerry spoke of "the tragedy" of Kobani, but nervously played down the significance of its capture. When a well-known Kurdish fighter, Arin Mirkan, blew herself up while surrounded by advancing ISIS fighters it looked like a sign of despair and impending defeat.

It also looked as if US plans to fight the Islamic State were in ruins as its fighters came close to capturing Kobani and had, in addition, inflicted a further heavy defeat on the Iraqi army west of Baghdad. The US-led air attacks launched against ISIS on August 8 in Iraq and September 23 in Syria were not as effective as expected and President Obama's plan to "degrade and destroy" the militants had not shown the first sign of success. In both Syria and Iraq, ISIS was still expanding its control rather than contracting.

ISIS reinforcements had been rushing toward Kobani in the effort to achieve a decisive victory over the town's remaining defenders. The jihadis were willing to take heavy casualties in street fighting and from air attacks in order to add to the string of victories they had won since they captured Mosul, the second largest city in Iraq, on June 10. Part of the strength of the fundamentalist movement is a sense that there is something inevitable and divinely inspired about its victories, whether it is against superior numbers in Mosul or US airpower at Kobani.

In the face of a likely ISIS victory at Kobani, senior US officials tried to explain away their nation's failure to save the town's Syrian Kurds, probably the jihadis' toughest opponents in Syria. "Our focus in Syria is in degrading the capacity of [the Islamic State] at its core to project power, to command itself, to sustain itself, to resource itself," said US deputy national security adviser Tony Blinken, in a typical piece of waffle designed to mask defeat. "The tragic reality is that in the course of doing that there are going to be places like Kobani where we may or may not be able to fight effectively."

It never happened: Washington could not allow ISIS another victory after Obama's rhetoric about degrading and destroying the movement. On October 19, US C-130 aircraft dropped twenty-one tons of arms and equipment to the rebels in Kobani to enable them to hold out. At the same time, the Turks appeared to reverse their previous hostility toward the Syrian Kurdish defenders at Kobani by announcing that they would allow a detachment of peshmerga to reinforce the beleaguered town.

At the time of writing, Kobani still has not fallen, though ISIS forces are entrenched in large parts of the town. Unfortunately for the US, it isn't the only place where air strikes are failing to stop the militants. In an offensive in Iraq launched on October 2 but little reported in the outside world, ISIS captured almost all the cities and towns it did not already hold in Anbar province, a vast area in western Iraq that makes up a quarter of the country. It had seized the city of Hit and much of the provincial capital Ramadi, which it had long fought for. Other cities, towns and bases on or close to the Euphrates River west of Baghdad fell in a few days, often after little resistance from the Iraqi Army, which proved as dysfunctional as ever, even with US air support. Soon only the city of Haditha and the Al-Asad military base near Hit were still in Iraqi government hands. In a study entitled "Iraq's Security Forces Collapse as the Islamic State Takes Control of Most of Anbar Province," Joel Wing concluded that "this was a huge victory for IS as it gives the insurgents virtual control over Anbar and poses a serious threat to western Baghdad."

The battle for Anbar, which was at the heart of the Sunni rebellion against the American occupation after 2003, has ended with a decisive victory for ISIS. It took large parts of Anbar in January and government counterattacks failed dismally with some 5,000 casualties in the first six months of the year. About half the province's 1.5 million population has fled and become refugees. The next target may be the Sunni enclaves of western Baghdad, starting with Abu Ghraib on the outskirts but leading right to the center of the capital.

The Iraqi government and its foreign allies are drawing comfort from the fact there have been some advances against ISIS in the center and the north of the country. But north and northeast of Baghdad the successes have not been won by the Iraqi army but by highly sectarian Shia militias that do not distinguish between ISIS and the rest of the Sunni population. They speak openly of getting rid of the Sunni in mixed provinces like Diyala. The result is that Sunnis in Iraq have no alternative but to stick with ISIS or flee, if they want to survive. The same is true northwest of Mosul on the border with Syria where Iraqi Kurdish forces aided by US air attacks have retaken the important border crossing of Rabia, but only one Sunni Arab remained in the town. Ethnic and sectarian cleansing has become the norm in the war in both Iraq and Syria.

The siege of Kobani has exposed the weakness of the US-led alliance opposing ISIS. At the start of the bombing in Syria, President Obama boasted of putting together a coalition of regional Sunni powers such as Turkey, Saudi Arabia, Qatar, Jordan, United Arab Emirates, and Bahrain, but these countries all have different agendas from that of the US, and destroying ISIS is not their first priority. The Sunni Arab monarchies may not like ISIS, which threatens the political status quo, but, as one Iraqi observer put it, "They like the fact that ISIS creates more problems for the Shia than it does for them."

Of the countries supposedly uniting on the American side, by far the most important is Turkey. It shares a 510-mile border with Syria across which Syrian rebels of all sorts, including ISIS and Jabhat al-Nusra, have passed with ease. This year the Turks have tightened up on border security, but since its successes in the summer ISIS no longer needs sanctuary, supplies, or volunteers from outside to the degree it once did. In the course of the siege of Kobani it became clear that Turkey considered the Syrian Kurdish political and military organizations the PYD (Democratic Union Party) and YPG (People's Protection Units) as posing a greater threat than the Islamic fundamentalists.

Moreover, the PYD is the Syrian branch of the Kurdistan Workers' Party (PKK), which has been fighting for Kurdish self-rule in Turkey since 1984. Ever since Syrian government forces withdrew from the Syrian Kurdish cantons on the border with Turkey in July 2012, Ankara has feared the impact of self-governing Syrian Kurds on its own fifteen-million-strong Kurdish population. President Erdoğan would clearly prefer ISIS to control Kobani rather than the PYD. When five PYD members, who had been fighting in Kobani, were picked up by the Turkish army as they crossed the border in October, they were denounced by as "separatist terrorists."

Turkey is demanding a high price from the US for its cooperation, such as a Turkish-controlled buffer zone inside Syria, where Syrian refugees are to live and anti-Assad rebels are to be trained. Erdoğan would like a no-fly zone, which would be another move against the government in Damascus since ISIS has no air force. If implemented, the plan would mean Turkey, backed by the US, would enter the Syrian civil war on the side of the rebels, though the anti-Assad forces are dominated by ISIS and Jabhat al-Nusra, the al-Qaeda affiliate. The latter led an attack on the Syrian government–held provincial capital of Idlib on October 27 that almost succeeded and in which seventy government officers were summarily executed in their headquarters.

It is worth keeping in mind when looking at Turkey's plans that its actions in Syria since 2011 have been a self-defeating blend of imperial hubris and almost comic ineptitude. At the start of the uprising, it could have held the balance between the government and its opponents. Instead, it supported the militarization of the crisis, backed the jihadis, and assumed that Assad would soon be defeated. This did not happen, and what had been a popular uprising became dominated by sectarian warlords who flourished in conditions created by Turkey. Erdoğan at first seemed to assume that he could disregard the rage of the Turkish Kurds at what they see as his complicity with ISIS against the Syrian Kurds.

The peace process in Turkey that maintained a ceasefire with the PKK since 2013 is close to collapse. Why doesn't Ankara worry more about this? It may believe that the PKK is too heavily involved in fighting in Syria to resume a war on another front. On the other hand, if Turkey does join the civil war in Syria against Assad, a crucial ally of Iran, then Iranian leaders have said that

"Turkey will pay a price." This probably means that Iran will covertly support an armed Kurdish insurgency in Turkey. One Iraqi politician commented: "The Iranians have a PhD in this type of warfare." Saddam Hussein made a somewhat similar mistake to Erdoğan's when he invaded Iran in 1980, thus leading Iran to reignite the Kurdish rebellion that Baghdad had crushed through an agreement with the shah in 1975. Turkish military intervention in Syria would not end the war there, but it might well spread the fighting to Turkey.

In attacking Kobani, the ISIS leadership wanted to prove that it could go on defeating its enemies, despite the US airstrikes. ISIS fighters defiantly chanted, "The Islamic State remains, the Islamic State expands," as they poured into Kobani to replace heavy losses. In the past, ISIS had been tactically agile in breaking off battles it did not think it was going to win, withdrawing from half of the territory it held in Syria in the face of an anti-ISIS rebel offensive in the first half of 2014. But the five-week battle for Kobani probably went on too long and was too well publicized for its militants to withdraw without loss of prestige. The appeal of the Islamic State to Sunni Muslims in Syria, Iraq, and across the world comes in part from a sense that its victories are God-given and inevitable, so any failure damages its claim to divine support.

The final ISIS victory at Kobani that seemed inevitable in early October had not happened at the end of the month, though the militants claimed they were simply mopping up the remaining pockets of resistance. The group was clearly suffering heavy losses in street fighting and from US air strikes. The delivery of arms and equipment to the Syrian branch of the PKK boosted the Kurds' military strength and morale. The White House became more impatient with Turkey's ill-concealed preference for ISIS over the Kurds.

Previously, ISIS commanders had been skillful in dispersing their men and hiding their equipment. By October 23, the air campaign of the US-led coalition had sent out 6,600 missions, but of these only 632, or just 10 percent of the total, resulted in air strikes against targets on the ground. But, in seeking to storm Kobani, ISIS military leaders had to concentrate their forces in identifiable positions and became vulnerable to attack. In one forty-eight-hour period there were forty US air strikes, some only fifty yards from the Kurdish front line.

Air strikes might block ISIS from overrunning Kobani, as they could feasibly do in Erbil or even Baghdad, but even this result was in doubt. There are limits to what an air campaign can achieve. The Islamic State was still expanding in October despite American military intervention. The US was still balking at giving military assistance to those who were fighting ISIS, such as the Syrian army, when it was supposedly still trying to overthrow Assad but, if the US had been serious about combating the extremist jihadis, then it would have realized it had little alternative. ISIS has many enemies, so numerous indeed that they should be able to overwhelm it in the long term, but their disunity and differing agendas mean that the Islamic State is fast becoming an established geographic and political fact on the map.

October 2014

Acknowledgements

This book was originally conceived as a description of the growing power of jihadi movements similar to al-Qaeda in northern Syria and Iraq, the importance of which seemed to me to have been missed by Western politicians, the media, and the public. I particularly wanted to trace the swift rise of ISIS, the growing anger of the Sunni community in Iraq, and the government's inability to combat a powerful new insurgency. In Syria I wanted to stress that the armed opposition was now dominated by jihadi movements while the moderates, whom the West is seeking to boost, have little influence on the ground.

What seemed a marginal opinion in 2013 and early 2014 was borne out by ISIS's capture of Mosul on June 10, 2014, and its declaration of a caliphate spanning the Iraqi-Syrian border later that month. The main conclusions of this book, written beforehand, seemed to be spectacularly confirmed by these events. But the war is not over and the battle lines will move backward and forward. Many players inside and outside the country are involved and Iraq and Syria have a way of delivering unexpected events and nasty surprises.

I developed many of the themes in this book while giving lectures for Alwan for the Arts Foundation in New York in 2014, as well as in articles for the *Independent* and the *London Review of Books*. Many thanks to all for their encouragement and support.

Index

9/11 4, 52, 53, 55, 56, 57, 59, 98, 100, 101, 102, 114, 116, 138
al-Abadi, Haider xv, 24
Abbottabad (Pakistan) 56
Abu Ghraib 46, 74, 147, 155
Adhamiya (Iraq) 20
al-Adnani, Abu Mohammed 18, 64, 76
Afghanistan 6, 8, 54, 59, 62, 98, 100, 104, 111–13, 115, 116, 138, 144
Ahfad al-Rasoul Brigade 85
Ahrar al-Sham 46, 51, 82, 84, 86, 148
Ajdabiya (Libya) 118
al-Ajmi, Nayef 106
Alawites x, 49, 81, 89, 91, 94, 98, 104, 132,

Aleppo (Syria) ix, xviii, 6, 33, 51, 82, 93, 149, 151
Allawi, Ali 108–9
Alwiyah Club 33
Amariya (Iraq) 21
Amerli (Iraq) xv, xviii
Anbar province (Iraq) 14, 21, 26, 47, 48, 74–5, 128, 129, 136, 154–5
Ansar al-Islam 14
Arab Spring 69, 83, 116, 126, 132, 139
Al-Asad base 154
Asaib Ahl al-Haq xiii
al-Askari 13, 70
al-Assad, Bashar xii, xvii, xix–xx, 3–4, 9, 26, 33–4, 37–8, 49, 52, 71,

84, 86–90, 92–3, 98–9, 103–5,
109–10, 112, 117, 130, 140,
142–3, 148, 157–8, 161
anti- xii, xix–xx, 3, 4, 52, 86–7,
98, 109–10, 148, 157
pro- xvii, 71, 89, 93
al-Assad, Hafez 143
al-Attiyah, Ghassan 67
"Awakening" movement 73, 128
ayatollah *see* Khomeini *and*
al-Sistani, Ali

Baathist party 14, 30, 31, 53, 142
Bab Touma (Syria) 121
Baghdad (Iraq) xii–xix, 1, 4, 9,
12–16, 18–21, 24–6, 28–9, 30,
32–4, 38–9, 42, 47–8, 61, 65–6,
70, 113–14, 116, 122, 124–6, 128,
145–7, 151, 152, 154–5, 159–60
conditions in xii–xiii, 4, 19–21,
26, 28–9, 32–3, 66, 70, 113–4
al-Baghdadi, Abu Bakr xi, 43–5, 135
Bahrain 7, 83, 103, 105, 108, 116,
126, 156
Baiji (Iraq) 17
Baquba (Iraq) 14
Barzani, Massoud 15, 32
Basra (Iraq) 46, 65, 123
al-Beilawy, Abdul-Rahman 129
Beirut (Lebanon) 133
Benghazi (Libya) 118
Biden, Joe xix–xx
bin Abdullah, Miteb 105
bin Laden, Osama 1, 4–5, 38, 54–7,
98, 100

bin Nayef, Mohammed 105
bin Sultan, Bandar 36, 86, 104, 105
bin Sultan, Salman 86
bin Zayed, Abdullah 102
Blundy, David 124
Boko Haram 109
Britain xiii, 6, 23, 27, 38, 42, 53, 59,
66, 86, 92, 119, 143
Bucca, Camp (Iraq) 44
Bush, George W. 56, 106

Cairo (Egypt) 132
caliphate xi, xvii, 27, 28, 30, 32, 38,
40, 164
Camp Bucca (Iraq) 44
Canada 42, 133
Chechnya 42, 51
China 141
Christians x, 5, 31, 49, 75, 81, 89,
91–2, 107–8, 121–2, 127, 151
Clapper, James 104
Clinton, Hillary 57, 101
Cohen, David 106
Colvin, Marie 106
Cuba 143

Daash 16
Damascus (Syria) 26, 33, 51, 52, 79,
80, 82, 89, 90, 91, 98, 121, 123,
124, 140, 157
Dawa party 24
Dearlove, Richard 35
Deir Ezzor (Syria) 27, 50
Diyala province (Iraq) 42, 44, 155
al-Dohra power station 125

Douma (Syria) 79
Dubai (UAE) 128

Egypt 42, 83, 103, 105, 113, 117,
126, 127, 130, 132, 141, 144, 149
Erbil (Iraq) xi, xii, xvi, 31, 34, 35,
137, 160
Erdoğan, Recep Tayyip 152, 157,
158, 159
El Salvador 124
Euphrates 12, 42, 48, 50, 74, 88,
124, 154
Europe xv, 4, 5, 9, 52, 57, 99, 109,
117, 140

Fallujah (Iraq) 1, 19, 24, 25, 48, 61,
62, 74, 126, 131, 135–6, 146
Fatimid dynasty 103
France 72, 86, 119
Free Syrian Army (FSA) 35, 51, 85,
90, 98,

Gaddafi, Muammar 54, 88, 112, 113,
117, 119–20, 142, 143
Germany 94, 109
Ghaidan, Ali 15
Gharawi, Mahdi 15

Hamada, Wael 80
al-Hamadi, Nazem 80
Hawijah (Iraq) 47, 74
Hezbollah 9, 71, 89, 92, 103
Holbrooke, Richard C. 5
Homs (Syria) 33, 81, 82, 89, 90, 93,
97, 121, 149

Hussein, Saddam x, xiii, 18, 30, 33,
44, 46, 53, 65–7, 69, 76, 100, 112,
115, 117, 142, 144, 146–8, 159
era 18, 30, 44, 46, 65, 76
invasion of Iran 159
invasion of Kuwait x, 147–8
overthrow of xiii, 33, 46, 66, 69,
100, 112
representation of 115
ties to 9/11 53, 100
Hussein, Safa Rusoul 21, 145

Indonesia 6
Institute for the Study of War 46,
73
International Crisis Group 69, 83,
84, 141
Inter-Services Intelligence 57–8
Iran x, xiii–xv, 9, 16, 30, 71, 92,
94–5, 100, 102–3, 110, 145, 148,
155, 158–9
as unlikely US ally x, xiv–xv
and Turkey 158–9
backing Assad xv, 9, 92, 94,
103, 155
influence in Iraq xiii, xiv, xv, 16,
30, 71, 145, 159
revolution 100
Iraq ix–xx, 1, 2, 4, 7–18, 23–39,
42–51, 53, 55, 57, 59, 61–77,
87–8, 94, 97–8, 100–3, 108–9,
111–17, 120–29, 131, 135–8, 141,
142, 144–50, 152–6, 159, 163–4
and Iran xiii, xiv, xv, 16, 30, 71,
145, 159

armed forces xi, xii, xiii, xvi,
    xvii, 11, 13–18, 25, 27, 29, 32,
    37, 44, 47–9, 62, 64–5, 75–7,
    112, 114–15, 128–9, 136–7,
    144–6, 151, 152, 154–5
corruption in 11–12, 29, 64–8,
    77, 136–7
destabilization of x, xiii–xiv,
    4, 8–10, 32–3, 73, 137, 144,
    147, 150
al-Qaeda in (former name of
    ISIS) 9, 11–12, 41, 42, 44–5,
    73, 135
ISIS in ix, x–xi, xix–xx, 9, 13,
    16–18, 21, 23, 25–7, 32, 36,
    37–8, 43–5, 48–50, 53, 61–77,
    87, 98, 129, 131, 136–7,
    145–6, 151, 154, 156, 159
media in 113–15, 116, 123, 125,
    128–31
Shia government of xvi–xvii,
    16, 18, 24, 33, 39, 47, 69–71,
    102–3, 149
Sunni resurgence in 61–77
war in x, xi, xii, xv, xvi, 4, 8, 9,
    23–5, 34–5, 38, 44, 48–9, 53,
    55, 57, 59, 61–77, 100–1, 111,
    112, 114–15, 116, 120, 125–7,
    138, 142, 144, 152, 154–6
al-Issawi, Rafi 62
ISIS ix, xiv, xv, 1–21, 23–5, 27–8,
    31–6, 37–9, 41–2, 44–53, 61–62,
    64, 69, 71–2, 74–7, 84–6, 88,
    92–3, 97–8, 128–31, 135–7, 139,
    145–6, 148, 150–61, 163–4

and al-Qaeda 11–12, 41, 43–5,
    52, 86
and JAN 50, 86
instilling fear x, xix, 2, 17, 31,
    34, 35, 38, 39, 41–2, 49, 75,
    97–8, 129–30, 152
guerrilla warfare xii, 23, 25, 145
new state 27–8, 38, 40, 160
obtaining arms 3, 37, 72
origins x, 8, 9, 77
rise of 1–10
seizing oil/gas fields 26, 37, 50
success of ix–xi, xvi–xx, 1–11,
    13–15, 18, 25–7, 33–6, 38,
    42, 45–50, 61, 62, 64, 69,
    71, 74–7, 84, 88, 92, 128–9,
    131, 135–7, 146, 148, 150–2,
    154–5, 156, 159–61, 164
underestimation of 28–30, 48
Islamic Front 50
Israel 26, 143

Jabhat al-Nusra (JAN) xix, 3, 23,
    26, 27, 35, 37, 43, 45, 46, 50, 51,
    53, 80, 82, 87, 89, 92, 93, 106,
    148, 156, 157
al-Jamal, Saddam 85–6
Jews 5, 107, 109, 127, 130
Jordan 7, 42, 52, 85, 87, 131, 156

Kabul (Afghanistan) 6, 113, 124
Kandahar (Afghanistan) 113
al-Kasir, Hila 36
Kerry, John 104, 152
al-Khalifa family 103, 108

al-Khalil, Samira 80
al-Khoei, Yousef 107
Khomeini (Ayatollah) 100
Kiev (Ukraine) 132
King Abdullah 102, 105, 106
Kirkuk (Iraq) xii
Kobani (Syria) xix, 13, 27, 151,
    152–4, 156–7, 159–60
Krak des Chevaliers (Syria) 90, 91
Kufa (Iraq) 124
Kurdistan ix, xi, xiv, 13, 15, 17, 67,
    75, 157
Kurdistan Workers' Party (PKK)
    157, 158, 160
Kurds ix–ii, xiv, xiv–xvii, xix, 13–5,
    24–5, 27, 31–2, 34–5, 37, 46, 49,
    69, 73, 91, 144, 147, 151–60
    ISIS assaults on, ix, xi, xiv, xv–
        xvi, 13, 25, 27, 35, 152–3
Kuwait 9, 105, 120, 130, 144, 148

Lashkar-e-Taiba 101
Latakia province (Syria) 42, 51, 149
Lebanon 7, 33, 71, 81, 91, 94, 121,
    143, 147, 148
Levey, Stuart 101
Lewis, Jessica D. 46, 73
Libya 8, 53, 83, 88, 111–13, 116,
    117–20, 131, 132, 141
Lloyd George, David 143

Maidan (Ukraine) 132
al-Maliki, Nouri xiii, xv, xvi, 9,
    15–16, 18, 24, 28, 30, 31, 32, 39,
    47, 63, 68, 71, 72, 76, 102, 137, 146

Maronites 91
al-Masmoudi, Waleed bin
    Muhammad al-Hadi 131
Mexico 132
Mirkan, Arin 152
Morocco 37, 51
Mosul (Iraq) x, xiv, xvii, 1, 4, 7,
    11–21, 25, 27, 30–1, 32, 35,
    38–40, 43, 46, 47, 49, 59, 64,
    75–6, 126, 129, 136–7, 138, 151,
    153, 155, 164
    Battle of 11–21
Moujahideen Army 14
Mubarak, Hosni 140
Mukhabarat police 139, 141
Mukhtar 75
Muslim Brotherhood 105

Nabq (Syria) 90
al-Najdi, Khatab 36
Naqshbandi 14
Nasser 117, 144
NATO 54, 58, 88, 112
Nineveh Operations 15
Nubl (Syria) 93, 149
al-Nusra *see* Jabhat al-Nusra

Obama, Barack xvi, 2–3, 7, 56, 57,
    104, 152, 153, 156
Othman, Mahmoud 77
Ottoman Empire 143

Pakistan 43, 57, 98, 100, 102, 138
    as US ally 4, 58, 100
    backing jihadi groups 5, 58, 138

Palestine 26

Palmyra (Syria) 27

peshmerga xiv, xvi, 15, 34, 151, 154

al-Qaeda xx, 1–6, 7, 9, 11–12, 27, 31, 38, 41–6, 48, 51–9, 73, 82, 86–7, 92, 98–9, 100–1, 104–6, 109, 127–8, 135, 138, 148, 157
  –type groups 1, 7, 9, 42, 43, 51, 52, 56, 59, 92, 109, 148
  in Iraq (former name of ISIS) 9, 11–12, 41, 42, 44, 45, 73, 135
  narrow focus on 52–6

al-Qahtani, Abdullah Azam Salih 131

Qalamoun Mountains (Syria) 33, 89

Qanbar, Abboud 15

Qatar 3, 7, 9, 34, 35, 50, 72, 82, 85, 99, 103, 105, 148, 156

Rabia (Iraq) 155

Ramadi (Iraq) 14, 15, 74, 154

Raqqa (Syria) 1, 36, 46, 87, 88

Rouhani, Hassan 71, 145

Russia 9, 26, 71, 92, 94, 95, 103

al-Saadi, Abdul Malik 75

al-Sadr, Muqtada xiii

Safavids 16, 25

Sahwa 73

Saladin 103

Salah ad-Din province (Iraq) 13, 63, 128–9

Salafi 81, 82, 87, 98, 99, 104

Saleh, Yassin al-Haj 80

Samarra (Iraq) 13, 44, 70

Saqlawiyah (Iraq) 25

Saudi Arabia x, xix, 3–9, 26, 34–7, 41, 52, 56–8, 69, 71, 72, 85, 86, 87, 92, 94, 95, 98–102, 104–10, 128, 130, 131, 138, 148, 156
  as US ally 4, 56–8, 100–2, 104–6
  backing jihadi groups 4–5, 26, 36, 52, 56, 57, 58, 72, 85, 98–100, 104, 138
  open border with Syria 36–7
  pulling back from jihadi groups 105–110
  Wahhabism in 5–6, 36, 72, 99, 100, 107–8

al-Shaer gas field 26

sharia 5, 50, 54, 84

Sharif, Nawaz 138

Shia x, xiii–xv, xvii–xix, 5–6, 13, 15–20, 24–5, 28–34, 36, 39, 47–8, 54, 57, 68–71, 73, 76, 86, 93–4, 97–100, 102–3, 107–9, 124, 127–30, 136, 138, 145–7, 149, 155–6
  and Kurds 31–2
  persecution of 57, 76, 97–8, 102–3, 107–9, 129, 130
  ISIS assaults on xv, 13, 17
  militias xiii, xiv–xv, xvii, 124, 155

Sinai (Egypt) 127

al-Sistani, Ali 29, 70

Soviet Union 100, 143–4

Stevens, Chris 54

Sufi 5, 107, 127
Sunni ix–x, xiii–xiv, xvi–xix, 6,
    8–9, 12–14, 16–21, 24, 26,
    29–33, 35–36, 38–40, 43–49, 57,
    61–77, 84, 86, 90–92, 94, 97–99,
    103–104, 107–109, 124, 126–129,
    132, 136–137, 144–147, 150,
    155–6, 159, 163
    and Wahhabism 6, 9
    Gulf monarchies x, 8, 156
    paramilitary groups 14
    resurgence in Iraq 61–77
    situation in Iraq xvi–xviii,
        19–20, 24, 39–40, 62–3,
        68–70, 155
    uprising ix, 9, 16, 32, 44, 45,
        47
    victims of Shia militias xiii,
        13–14
Syria ix–xii, xiv–xv, xvii–xx, 1–4,
    7–10, 12–4, 24–8, 33–8, 41–7,
    49–53, 71–3, 79–95, 97–9,
    103–6, 108–14, 116–17, 121–5,
    127, 129–33, 135, 137–8, 140–5,
    147–9, 151–61, 163–4
    conditions in x, xvii, xviii, xx,
        1–3, 7, 9, 10, 25–7, 33–8,
        41–7, 49–53, 71–2, 79–84,
        89–95, 97–8, 103–4, 108–10,
        114, 121–5, 129, 130–3, 135,
        140–4, 147–9, 153–6
    ISIS assaults on ix, xi, xii, xviii–
        xix, 13, 25, 26, 27, 33, 36, 46,
        47, 131–2, 148, 151, 153–4,
        159–61

government forces xvii, xviii,
    33, 82, 87–91, 121, 148, 151,
    161
inter-rebel civil war xii, xviii, 46,
    50, 86, 87–8, 91
opposition groups 3, 34, 49, 51,
    72, 73, 84, 85, 86, 98, 103–6,
    109, 130–1, 135, 142, 149,
    151, 157, 163
uprising 33, 44, 45, 47, 69,
    79–95, 137

Tabqa (Syria) xviii
Tahrir Square (Egypt) 132
Taji prison 74
Taliban 5, 54, 58, 62, 85, 98, 101,
    102, 104, 112, 113, 115
Tal Kalakh (Syria) 121
al-Tamimi, Aymenn 30, 34
Tigris 12, 20, 41, 42
Tikrit (Iraq) xiv, 1, 13, 17, 18, 19,
    25, 29, 39, 43, 49, 63, 129
Thirty Years' War 94
Tunisia 6, 83, 87, 126, 131
Turkey xix, 7, 9, 34, 35, 37, 42, 50,
    51, 69, 77, 82, 86, 92, 103, 141,
    148, 151, 152, 154, 156, 157,
    158–9, 160

United Arab Emirates xix, 7, 9, 34,
    85, 102, 105, 156
United States x–xvi, xviii–xx, 1–4,
    7–9, 12, 14–15, 18, 23–7, 33–5,
    37–8, 44–6, 48, 52–9, 66–7,
    70–1, 73, 77, 86–7, 92, 94–5,

100–2, 104–6, 114–16, 119, 126,
138, 143–6, 148, 150, 152–7,
159–61
and Assad xix–xx, 3, 8, 26, 52,
86–7, 92, 105, 161
and Iran x, xiv–xv, 100
and Saudi Arabia 4, 7, 56–7,
58, 86, 94, 100–2, 104, 105,
106, 138
attacks on ISIS x, xi–xii, xv,
xvi, xviii, 7, 23–4, 25, 27,
34–5, 37, 146, 152–3, 156,
159, 160
backing rebel groups 26, 33–4,
52–3, 54, 73, 161
in Iraq x–xvi, 1, 8, 9, 14, 24, 25,
33, 34, 42, 44, 45, 48, 53, 59,
66, 67, 70, 114–16, 124, 126,
138, 143, 146, 152–6
"troop surge" xvi, 12

Vietnam 143
Visser, Reidar 24

al-Waer (Syria) 90
Wahhabism 4, 5–6, 9, 71, 99–100,
107–8, 109
war on terror 2–3, 4, 7, 8, 38, 56,
58, 59
Wing, Joel 154

Yarmouk Brigade 52–3
Yazidi xv, 34, 75, 151
Yemen 83, 127, 131
Younis (Jonah) shrine 36

Zahraa (Syria) 93, 149
Zaitouneh, Razan 79–80
Zardari, Asif Ali 102
al-Zarqawi, Abu Musab 42
al-Zawahiri, Ayman 43, 52
Zeidan, Ali 113
al-Zughbi, Mohammad 130